After the Rapture

Life in the New World

Raymond Schafer

with P. H. Johnston

Vision House Publishers
Santa Ana, California 92705

Except where otherwise indicated, all Scripture quotations are taken from the New American Standard Bible, Copyright ©The Lockman Foundation 1960, 1962, 1963, 1968, 1971. Used by permission.

Verses marked TLB are taken from The Living Bible, Copyright 1971 by Tyndale House Publishers, Wheaton, Illinois. Used by permission.

Verses marked KJV are taken from the King James Version.

Verses marked RKJV are taken from the Readable King James Version by Raymond Schafer.

After the Rapture

Library of Congress Catalog Card Number 77-71636
ISBN 0-88449-061-0

Printed in the United States of America.

Cover Photo by Raymond Schafer.

CONTENTS

Chapter 1

THE SHOUT!

The Lord Himself will descend from heaven with a shout, with the voice of the archangel and with the trumpet of God.

—1 Thessalonians 4:16

It's the shout!

All around the world millions of people look up in surprise at the shout from the sky. Dogs bark, conversation ceases, and sleeping people awake.

Another voice booms like thunder from the heavens, "Maranatha! The Lord has come back for His own!" A piercing trumpet call shatters the subsequent silence, and thousands more people look up in surprise.

Within seconds another trumpet call pierces the air, and millions of graves all over the world burst open in silent explosions. Seconds later, startled Christians from every country in the world feel the surge of fresh vigor in their suddenly transformed bodies.

"The Rapture! It's the Rapture!" The truth of the fact overwhelms the newly-transformed Christians as they anticipate the next thrilling moments of the Rapture. And now from the opened graves begin to appear long-departed fathers and grandmothers, relatives and children. The reunion is ecstatic as once-deceased believers glow with the glory of resurrection life. Once eaten by cancer, there stands Mother in all the beauty of youth! And long-mourned Baby, who died in infancy—here he now stands as a stunning young man!

The earthly Christians and their heavenly visitors embrace each other in a joyful fellowship of love, and soon the whole triumphant group starts rising hand-in-hand to the Lord of glory awaiting them in the clouds of the sky.

Too Good to Be True?

From the purely secular point of view, the above scenario is definitely too good to be true—just pie-in-the-sky wishful thinking. But from the factual viewpoint of God Himself, the above scenario is as true as the Bible itself. Though many authors have written about the Tribulation horrors which await unbelievers left behind at the Rapture, few have written about the thrills of eternal life which await Christ's believers after they are taken up to heaven by the miracle of the Rapture. This book seeks to correct that imbalance.

We would now like to introduce you to the after-the-Rapture experience in a way you may never have enjoyed before. May God give you the joy of heaven itself as you come with us into the adventure of God's new world. Though this book is based on a tremendous amount of Biblical research, its fast-moving style is designed especially for your reading enjoyment. If you would like to read still more about future events after finishing this book, refer to the Recommended Reading list on page 141.

How Soon?

Sometime before the year 55 A.D., Paul the Apostle wrote to Christ's new believers in the Grecian city of Thessalonica, "You turned to God from idols to serve a living and true God, and to wait for His Son from heaven, whom He raised from the dead, that is, Jesus, who delivers us from the wrath to come."[1] Later Paul wrote to the Philippian believers, "Our citizenship is in heaven, from which also we eagerly wait for a Savior, the Lord Jesus Christ."[2] Paul's words were based on the words of Christ Himself, spoken just before the Savior died, rose, and went back to heaven: "In My Father's house are many dwellingplaces; if it were not so I would have told you, for I go to prepare a place for you. And if I go and prepare a place for you, I will come again and receive you to Myself, that where I am you may be also."[3]

How soon can Christ come to the clouds to take us back to heaven with Himself? Listen to these words of Jesus, spoken to Peter in the presence of John in about the year 30 A.D.: "If I want him to remain until I come, what is that to you? *You* follow Me!"[4] Jesus said He could have come back within the lifetime of John the Apostle! Today we know that Jesus *didn't* come back that soon, but we also

---

All footnotes are listed at the back of this book, beginning on page 143.

know that His coming for us is nearer than ever,[5] and that today may be the very day we hear His shout in the sky.

Some Thessalonian believers needed to be told to keep working until Christ returns at the Rapture, and perhaps some of us also need to be told to "occupy till He comes."[6] But most of us probably need to be reminded instead that Christ said, "Surely I come quickly."[7] And all of us need to respond, "Even so come, Lord Jesus."[8] Just think of it—if we know Christ as our Savior we may no longer be in this world 24 hours from now!

What a Way to Go!

"We do not want you to be uninformed," wrote Paul, "about those who are asleep, that you may not grieve, as do the rest, who have no hope. For if we believe that Jesus died and rose again, even so God will bring with Him those who have fallen asleep in Jesus. For we say to you by the word of the Lord that we who are alive and remain until the coming of the Lord shall not precede those who have fallen asleep. For the Lord Himself will descend from heaven with a shout, with the voice of the archangel, and with the trumpet of God, and the dead in Christ shall rise first. Then we who are alive and remain shall be caught up together with them in the clouds to meet the Lord in the air, and thus we shall always be with the Lord. Therefore comfort one another with these words."[9]

We've often been told that the entire Rapture

will take place "in the twinkling of an eye," yet the verses just quoted (1 Thessalonians 4:13-18), when compared with 1 Corinthians 15:51-53, show that while *the transformation of the bodies of living believers* will take place in the twinkling of an eye, *the Rapture as a whole* will be a majestic sequence of events that takes place over a period of several seconds or longer. The original Greek wording of 1 Thessalonians 4:16, 17 and 1 Corinthians 15:51-53 shows the following beautiful order of events at the time of the Rapture:

1) Christ's descent from heaven with a shout (1 Thess. 4:16a)
2) The voice of the archangel (1 Thess. 4:16b)
3) The first trumpet call (1 Thess. 4:16c)
4) The second trumpet call and the bodily transformation of heavenly and earthly believers (1 Thess. 4:16d; 1 Cor. 15:51, 52)
5) The brief reunion of heavenly and earthly believers (required by the Greek wording of 1 Thess. 4:17)[10]
6) The ascension to the clouds by heavenly and earthly believers as a fellowshiping group (1 Thess. 4:17).

First Thessalonians 4:17 says literally, "together with them we will be caught up in the clouds to meet the Lord in the air." What a beautiful way to go to heaven! First we will enjoy a quick reunion with our Christian loved ones, whether still alive or once-deceased, and then hand-in-hand we will rise to the clouds with our eternal companions of glory!

Heavenly Rendezvous

When we reach the clouds we'll meet the Lord at some geographical point which is central to believers from all over the globe (so that all Christians in the world can travel to heaven in a single large group, with Christ as their Leader). To see Christ in person should and will be the pinnacle in the career of every Christian on earth. With Thomas of old we'll shout, "My Lord and my God!"[11] Tears of joy and gratitude will flow from our resurrection faces as we look at that tender, manly face that still glows with the sacrificial love of Calvary. No pierced hands or feet will ever have looked more beautiful to men or angels. With the songwriter we'll sing,

> Majestic sweetness sits enthroned
> upon the Savior's brow—
> His head with radiant glories crowned,
> His lips with grace o'erflow.
>
> To Him I owe my life and breath,
> and all the joys I have;
> He makes me triumph over death,
> and saves me from the grave.[12]

The trip to heaven will be a joyous one. On the way we'll talk with the Savior Himself. Later we'll talk about our past experiences of earth and the unfolding joys of heaven, but for the moment the Lord Jesus Christ Himself will be the center of attraction for every Christian in that resurrected crowd on its way to heaven. Eternity itself will hardly be long enough to adequately praise the triumphant Redeemer of men.

Raptured Babies?

How about the babies? Will they also be caught up at the Rapture? Second Samuel 12:23, Mark 10:14-16, and Luke 18:16 seem to indicate that all people who die in infancy or young childhood will automatically be taken to heaven on the basis of Christ's substitutionary death at Calvary. If this is true about *deceased* babies (and we believe it is), then will *living* babies and young children automatically be taken up to heaven at the time of the Rapture?

We believe they will. The Bible mentions not a single word about children being on earth during the Tribulation period following the Rapture, except for babies newly born near the end of this terrible seven-year period.[13] This strengthens our belief that *all* young children, whether of believing or unbelieving parents, will be taken up to heaven at the time of the Rapture. This sudden disappearance of the babies may be why Paul warns us in 1 Thessalonians 5:2-4, "You yourselves know full well that the day of the Lord will come just like a thief in the night. While they are saying, 'Peace and safety!' then destruction will come upon them suddenly . . . and they shall not escape. But you, brethren, are not in darkness, that the day should overtake you like a thief."

From the point of view of the people left behind on earth, the Rapture will be one of the greatest traumas in all of human history. Many of the very best adult citizens on earth will suddenly and mysteriously be gone, and every baby and young child in the world will unexplainably be gone with them. What a day of anguish for the world of unbelievers left behind at the Rapture!

No Second Chance?

How about the horror-stricken people left behind on the earth? Will any of these still be able to receive Christ as their Savior? Even though Revelation 7:4-10 tells us that millions of people in the post-Rapture world will turn to Christ for salvation, 2 Thessalonians 2:8-12 warns us that millions of others will be doomed to Satanic deception and eternal condemnation because they refused to receive the truth about Christ when they had the opportunity to do so.

So who can get saved after the Rapture? Apparently only those people who never clearly understood the good news about Christ *before* the Rapture. For those who knew about Christ but rejected Him before the Rapture, their fate is apparently sealed forever once the Rapture has taken place: "God will send upon them a deluding influence, so that they might believe what is false, in order that they all may be judged who did not believe the truth, but took pleasure in wickedness."[14]

Today is our finest opportunity to turn to Jesus Christ as our personal Savior and Friend. Tomorrow may be too late, since none of us knows what tomorrow will bring, or even how this very day will end. "Today if you hear God's voice, do not harden your heart."[15]

Chapter 2

FOREVER YOUNG

As we have borne the image of the earthy, we shall also bear the image of the heavenly.

—1 Corinthians 15:49

From the dawn of human history men have longed for the secret of eternal youth—for the power to live on forever in healthy young bodies. In 1513 Ponce de Leon crossed the ocean in quest of the fountain of youth, but instead he discovered the territory which we now call Florida. Millions of men before and after Ponce de Leon have searched for the key to endless life, but most of them have searched in vain because they have rejected the one true Source of eternal life in all the universe.

The patriarch Job, however, found that one Source of life. Over four thousand years ago he cried out, "For I know that my Redeemer lives, and that He shall stand at the latter day upon the earth. And though my skin is destroyed, yet in my flesh shall I see God, whom I shall see for myself, and mine eyes shall behold, and not another."[1] Grieving Martha also knew that one Source of life, for she said to Jesus about deceased Lazarus, "I know that he will rise again in the resurrection on the last day."[2] The permanent bodily resurrection of Christ was also well-known to King David of ancient times, for he predicted of the coming Messiah, "Neither wilt Thou allow Thy Holy One to undergo decay."[3] And Daniel the prophet predicted of the people in the end times, "Many of those who sleep in the dust of the ground will awake."[4]

Lifetime Guarantee

Who is this one true Source of eternal life? It is Jesus Christ Himself. As Paul the Apostle said in 1 Corinthians 15:20, 22, "Christ has been raised from the dead, the firstfruits of those who are asleep. . . . For as in Adam all die, so also in Christ all shall be made alive." Even though Lazarus, the widow's son, and several other Bible personalities came back from the dead before the resurrection of Christ,[5] none of these people enjoyed a permanent physical resurrection in the Biblical sense of the word, since as far as we can tell the bodies of all these people grew old and died again.

Resurrection in the New Testament sense of the word means that we will get a glorious new body that can walk forever on the streets of either heaven or earth. This was the kind of body Christ received when He rose from the dead nearly two thousand years ago, and this is the kind of body we will receive when the trumpet sounds at the time of the Rapture. No wonder the resurrection of Christ has been worth celebrating for nearly two thousand years in a row!

In addition to being the best-attested personal event of ancient history, Christ's resurrection establishes the foundation on which our own resurrection is based. As Paul said in Romans 4:25, Christ "was delivered up because of our transgressions and was raised because of our justification." Christ's resurrection proved that God was fully satisfied with the sacrificial death that Christ died on the Cross on our behalf, and that from now on everyone who turns to Christ in faith will receive full forgiveness of his sins and the guarantee of a beautiful new body at the time of the Rapture.

The sequence of "Christ's resurrection first, then ours" is pictured beautifully in the farmer's first harvest and later crops: "Each in his own order: Christ the firstfruits, after that those who are Christ's at His coming."[6] Just as the firstfruits of a healthy crop indicate that more harvest will soon follow, so Christ's resurrection shows that our own resurrection is not far behind.

Like the Stars

A grain of wheat is not a particularly beautiful thing to look at unless we examine it carefully under a microscope, yet the golden heads of grain waving gently in the sunset are beautiful indeed. This is a faint picture of what our resurrection bodies will be like. "That which you sow, you do not sow the body which is to be, but a bare grain, perhaps of wheat or of something else. But God gives it a body just as He wished, and to each of the seeds a body of its own. . . . So also is the resurrection of the dead. It is sown a perishable body, it is raised an imperishable body; it is sown in dishonor, it is raised in glory; it is sown in weakness, it is raised in power; it is sown a natural body, it is raised a spiritual body. If there is a natural body, there is also a spiritual body."[7]

Just as Adam brought a curse upon all men, so Christ promises a glorious new resurrection body to all people who take Him as their Savior. In the words of the Bible, "The first man is from the earth, earthy; the second man is from heaven. As is the earthy, so also are those who are earthy; and as is the heavenly, so also are those who are heavenly. And just as we have borne the image of the earthy, we shall also bear the image of the heavenly."[8]

Until telescopes were invented in the 1600's, people thought the stars were just cute little specks twinkling in the sky. But when astronomers started peering into the wonders of the galaxies, their opinion of the beauty of the stars was upgraded dramatically. Now for the first time they could see the spectacular glory of God's creation splashed across the expanses of space. To every thinking person today, the flaming color photos we see of God's fireworks in the sky make us cry out, "How great Thou art!" Yet this kind of beauty will be ours in our resurrection bodies: "There is one glory of the sun and another glory of the moon and another glory of the stars, for star differs from star in glory. So also is the resurrection of the dead."[9]

Daniel the prophet adds, "Those who have insight will shine brightly, like the brightness of the expanse of heaven, and those who lead the many to righteousness like the stars forever and ever."[10] Even though all of us will have glorious resurrection bodies, some of us will have even more glorious bodies than others, depending on how faithfully we've served the Lord during our time on earth. For example, people who have been willing to die rather than renounce their faith in Christ will receive especially beautiful resurrection bodies: "Others were tortured, not accepting their release, in order that they might obtain a better resurrection."[11] Yet we don't have to die as martyrs in order to enjoy a glorious resurrection experience at the time of the Rapture. Jesus Himself said, "Blessed are the pure in heart, for they shall see God. . . . Blessed are those who have been persecuted for the sake of righteousness, for theirs is the kingdom of heaven. . . . Rejoice and be glad, for your reward in heaven is great."[12]

In that day no one will be jealous of the greater glory of another resurrected believer, since everyone in heaven will realize that God has honored each believer with absolute fairness. Any regrets will be with ourselves alone,[13] for having neglected the Lord during our few short years on earth.

Thirty Forever

Our resurrection bodies will be designed to operate efficiently in *two* different environments—both heaven and earth—since we'll be visiting the earth frequently during Christ's thousand-year kingdom reign following the seven-year Tribulation period.[14] From various New Testament descriptions of Christ's resurrection body, it seems that both His own resurrection body and our new bodies will have *two* distinct modes or appearances. One mode will be the heavenly one, in which we will "shine like

17

the stars forever and ever,"[15] and the other mode will be the earthly one, in which we will look like ordinary human beings to the people who are living on the millennial earth.

This is exactly what Christ looked like to His followers during most of the times that He appeared to them after His resurrection. Through her tear-filled eyes Mary mistook Jesus for a healthy young gardener.[16] The two disciples who walked with Jesus to Emmaus mistook Him for a "stranger in Jerusalem."[17] The disciples in the early-morning mist of Lake Galilee didn't know who the lone figure on the shore was until John finally recognized His miraculous power and identified Him as the risen Christ.[18] When we visit earth people during Christ's thousand-year kingdom reign, we won't seem like gods from the sky to be praised or worshiped. Instead, we'll appear as the joyful people of God, willing to help God's citizens on earth in any way we can. The wonderful thing is that we'll be brilliant, young, and healthy forever.

To Mary, Jesus looked like a healthy young gardener, and perhaps that's a clue to our own eternal appearance as well. Your old and ailing mother will become a beautiful young woman forever. Your deceased baby will become that vigorous young man you once dreamed of rearing. And that retarded nephew—no longer will everyone pity him, for now he will become a leader of men. Even Uncle George, with his horrible war wounds, will possess a perfect new body that is marveled at by everyone.

Though we'll be able to pass through solid walls and ascend to heaven at will, even as Jesus did,[19] we'll also be able to walk, talk, and eat with the ordinary people of earth.[20] In those days we will eat neither out of necessity nor out of gluttony, but simply as a legitimate pleasure available to all of God's people.[21]

Will we recognize each other in heaven? Of course. The disciples' initial failure to recognize Jesus was only temporary, and after that they fellowshiped with Him as never before.[22] Every Christian you ever wanted to meet will be available for your eternal friendship and camaraderie. No prominent Christian leader will be too important to see you. You will have easy access to Paul, Moses, and Christ Himself. Every person you ever led to the Lord, even indirectly, will embrace you with the love of eternal life.[23] Every person in heaven, whether black or white, or rich or poor on earth, will be bound together by a fellowship of love that lasts forever.[24] "Baptist," "Brethren," "Presbyterian," or "Pentecostal" will mean nothing in heaven—every person there will just be a brother or sister in Christ![25]

Better than Sex

How about sex? Will this be a legitimate joy of heaven? Marriage was originally given by God to the human race for three reasons: to provide companionship,[26] to propagate the human race,[27] and, most important of all, to picture the heavenly marriage relationship between Christ and His redeemed people.[28] In other words, marriage here on earth is just a beautiful picture of what our spiritual union with Christ will be like in heaven. Marriage on earth can and should be a joyful, spiritually enriching experience, but our spiritual marriage with Christ in heaven will be by far the most intimate relationship of all time or eternity.

Jesus Himself said, "In the resurrection they neither marry nor are given in marriage, but are like angels in heaven."[29] There will be no sex activity in heaven, but we won't miss it because our beautiful relationship with Christ will completely eclipse even our most joyful moments of marriage here on earth.

But will men look like men, and women like women? Christ still looked like a man in His resurrection body,[30] and so will all the men who go to heaven. But how about the women? Though the Bible gives little explicit information on the appearance of resurrected women, it does give us some guiding principles. The creation of Eve was a holy act of God which took place before the sin of mankind.[31] Nowhere in the Bible is there any hint that a woman's femininity is an undesirable thing in the sight of God. It is true that God has given the role of church leadership and public teaching to men,[32] but it is also true that intrinsically "there is neither Jew nor Greek, there is neither slave nor free man, there is neither male nor female, for you are all one in Christ Jesus."[33]

We can see no Biblical reason at all why Christian women on earth today will stop being women in the resurrection. It's true that neither men nor women in heaven will participate in the propagation of children, but it is also true that men and women are distinct in many ways besides their basic reproductive systems! We believe that resurrected men will retain all their secondary sex characteristics, including masculine voice, muscular build, and facial and body hair, even as Christ apparently did in His own resurrection body.[34] Resurrected women, we believe, will look somewhat similar to the most beautiful women on earth today, except that their beauty will not be the object of sexual passions of any kind.

Will people in heaven wear clothing? We believe they will. We believe that the white clothing mentioned in Revelation 3:5; 4:4; 7:9, 13; 15:6; and 19:8, 14 indicates that the nudity of Adam and Eve, though perfectly proper before their sin,[35] will not be duplicated in heaven.

But these intriguing physical aspects of our resurrection bodies, though important, will not be nearly as important as our eternal spiritual companionship with our fellow believers and with Jesus Himself. We won't be fascinated so much by our own beauty as by the beauty of Christ Himself.[36] And of course this should be our prime fascination even while we're still here on earth:

> The bride eyes not her garment,
>   But her dear Bridegroom's face;
> We will not gaze at glory,
>   But on the King of grace![37]

All in the Family?

Will there be families in heaven, or will the Rapture be "the great divorce," alienating lifelong marriage partners and splitting happy families? Certainly there will be no hostility between any two people in heaven, for all of us will "love one another, for love is from God, and everyone who loves is born of God and knows God."[38]

Instead of *diminishing* friendships between family members, heaven will *increase* fellowship between all believers, whether of the same earthly family or not. Our friendships will be broadened immensely without jeopardizing our Christian love for the family members who go to heaven with us. For the first time all Christian men and women will be able to fellowship with each other as freely as they like, with no risk whatever of getting into moral trouble with each other. In one sense the broadened fellowship of heaven will be the greatest social emancipation of all time. No woman in heaven will ever again feel slighted, and no man will ever again be jilted by rejected love. No more battered children or inferiority complexes, and no more family arguments or "silent treatments." Never again will a wounded believer cry himself to sleep or suffer through years of humiliation and misunderstanding. In God's new world the sorrows of earth will be forgotten, and the joy of perfect living will sustain us forever.[39]

No, the real question is not whether there will be families in heaven, but whether we are right now members of God's redeemed family of love, waiting for the thrill of the Rapture. How do we enter this family of love? By receiving for ourselves the love which God offers us through the Lord Jesus Christ— by receiving Jesus as the Lover of our souls and the Savior from our sins.

Chapter 3

LIFE IN THE SKY

In My Father's house are many dwelling places . . . . I go to prepare a place for you.

—John 14:3

A thousand stars twinkled in the silent night sky over the ancient desert city. By now most of the merchants and tradesmen were asleep, but Abraham still pondered the quiet voice of God: "Go forth from your country and from your relatives and from your father's house to the land which I will show you; and I will make you a great nation, and I will bless you and make your name great, and so you shall be a blessing."[1]

Should Abraham really leave Haran, the city of his father and family? Here Abraham had already become a fairly wealthy merchant, but now God was asking him to leave. What better destination could God possibly have in mind than this comfortable center of family and friends? The question must have weighed heavily on the mind of godly Abraham.

Abraham the Alien

Abraham's decision is now a matter of history: "By faith Abraham, when he was called, obeyed by going out to a place which he was to receive for an inheritance, and he went out, not knowing where he was going."[2] The rest of Abraham's history on earth shows that God blessed him richly in several important respects—Abraham walked with God in a uniquely intimate fellowship, he became extremely wealthy, and he fathered Isaac, the forerunner of all Jewish people in the world.[3] But there was one thing Abraham never again enjoyed during his lifetime on earth, and that was the luxury of comfortable city living: "By faith he lived as an alien in the land of promise, as in a foreign land, dwelling in tents . . . for he was looking for the city which has foundations, whose architect and builder is God."[4]

Did Abraham ever receive that "city with foundations" built by God Himself? Listen to these words which describe Abraham and other people with similar faith: "They desire a better country, that is, a heavenly one. Therefore God is not ashamed to be called their God, for He has prepared [strong past tense] a city for them."[5] Did Abraham ever receive that city he was looking for? Yes, we believe he did, and so did thousands of other believers with him. In John 14:2 Jesus said to His disciples, "In My Father's house are many dwelling-places; if it were not so I would have told you, for I go to prepare a place for you." Eternal life in the Father's house, the city of God, is what we will describe in the remainder of this chapter.

City with Foundations

Except for people who happen to live in earthquake-prone areas of the world, most of us seem to feel that our cities are built on fairly solid foundations. Yet in reality it is the city of God in heaven which has the solid foundations, and it is our cities on earth which have the shaky ones, for after the seven-year Tribulation and thousand-year Millennium, God will destroy both earth and sky in an unprecedented holocaust of fire.[6] Yet after the fire, the city of God from heaven will emerge more beautiful than ever,[7] since this is the city with the truly eternal foundations.[8]

What is this city of God like? From the spiritual point of view, "you have come to Mount Zion and to the city of the living God, the heavenly Jerusalem, and to myriads of angels, to the general assembly and church of the firstborn who are enrolled in heaven, and to God the Judge of all, and to the spirits of righteous men made perfect, and to Jesus, the Mediator of a new covenant, and to the sprinkled blood, which speaks better than the blood of Abel."[9] God's city in heaven is a place of fellowship, worship, and joy, of "righteous men made perfect" and of Jesus Himself. There all the deepest longings of our heart will be satisfied as we sing,

> The bride eyes not her garment, but her
> dear Bridegroom's face;
>> I will not gaze at glory, but on my
>> King of grace—
> Not at the crown He giveth, but on His
> pierced hand;
>> The Lamb is all the glory
>> of Immanuel's Land![10]

All the worship that we ever wanted to give Christ but could never adequately express on earth will be fully expressed in heaven. Every newcomer to heaven will crowd around the Savior Himself, enthralled with the radiant warmth of the living Redeemer. Our bodies will be real, the people will be real, and the city itself will be real. Everything about heaven will be so beautifully tangible that we'll wonder why we ever balked at the thought of living forever in this beautiful place!

Yellowstone of the Sky

Abraham's heavenly home is not just a *city*, with ivory palaces and streets of gold,[11] but it is also a *country*, with scenic vistas of magnificent beauty. Abraham and his faith partners down through the ages have been "seeking a country [literally 'fatherland'] of their own. And indeed if they had been thinking of that country from which they went out, they would have had opportunity to return. But as it is, they desire a better country, that is, a heavenly one. Therefore God is not ashamed to be called their God, for He has prepared a city for them."[12]

If the city of Revelation 21 is essentially the same as the city to which we go at the time of the Rapture (and we believe it is), then our heavenly home is an immense place, larger than the entire western half of the United States![13] Will heaven be one vast urban complex? We think not. We think heaven will have its rolling hills and scenic mountains, quiet ponds and splashing waterfalls. We think heaven will have fragrant flowers and towering trees, photogenic beauty never equaled by earth's most scenic spots. We believe that no one in heaven will ever be able to say, "Yes, this place is lovely, but Yellowstone Park was better!" Keep in mind that the beauties of God's good earth are not sinful, but holy, and that someday the earth itself will be renewed into a beautiful millennial world.[14] Now and forever that flawless city in the sky will display all the beauties of the Creator Himself.

Pets in Paradise?

Will there be animals in heaven? We can't give a dogmatic answer to this question, but we do know that animals are an integral part of God's creative program on earth. God's creative order looks something like this:

Angels
People
Animals
Trees and plants
Inanimate objects (air, water, minerals, etc.)

We know that angels and people are inhabiting heaven already, and we know that heaven has (or will have) at least one fruit-bearing "tree of life" in it.[15] We also know that the heavenly city is (or will be) composed of a vast amount of gold and other precious minerals.[16] If the scope of God's handiwork is as complete in heaven as it is on earth, then heaven does indeed contain animals.

Will the animals in heaven serve as our pets? God clearly had pets in mind for the first two people

He created on earth: "Be fruitful and multiply, and
fill the earth and subdue it, and rule over the fish of
the sea and over the birds of the sky and over every
living thing that moves on the earth."[17] Not until
Adam and Eve sinned was there any fear or hostility
between animals and people. It's hard to prove
conclusively that there will be pets in heaven, but
we feel that their presence there would harmonize
well with the creatorial grandeur of God. Of course,
animals on *earth* will never make it to heaven, since
they are part of the groaning, dying creation described in Romans 8:20-22. If there are pets in
heaven they are perfect, undying animals which
never bite, scratch, or wet the floors. When Johnny
asks the question, "Mommy, will Scamper go to
heaven too?" perhaps the best answer would be,
"No, Johnny, Scamper won't be there, but maybe
there will be other animals in heaven which are even
better than Scamper!"

Talk to Your Angel

One of the great thrills of heaven will be to
meet the angels of God. Angels were apparently
created long before Adam and Eve, and most of
them have remained sinlessly faithful to God
through many thousands of years.[18] A large minority of angels, however, followed Lucifer (now Satan)
in rebelling against God, and were thereby ejected
from heaven. Many thousands of angels are now led
by Satan in hindering God's present program on
earth,[19] while other fallen angels are consigned to
eternal darkness.[20]

Contrary to popular misconceptions, the angels of God who commute between heaven and earth apparently have real, permanent bodies of approximately the same physical dimensions as those of a normal human male.[21] (But of course the angels who commute to earth keep their bodies invisible from earthly human beings most of the time.) The *fallen* angels have apparently been deprived of their bodies as part of their punishment for rebelling against their Creator. That is why these demons are constantly seeking idol statues, people, animals, or even plants or buildings in which to live.[22] When a fallen angel takes up residence in a human body, this is called demon possession, and it is a very real phenomenon in many parts of the world today.

Like humans, angels have spirits, souls, and bodies, and they exist forever.[23] Unlike humans, all angels are male in appearance, and no angels reproduce.[24] There are at least three distinct kinds of angels: cherubs (sometimes called cherubim), seraphs (sometimes called seraphim), and commuting angels. The cherubs have two wings and spend most or all of their time guarding the glory of God.[25] The seraphs have six wings and apparently specialize in worshiping the holy God of heaven.[26] The commuting angels are basically human in appearance and are the ones most often mentioned in the Bible (over five hundred times). It is the job of the commuting angels to guard little children and to serve the people of God generally.[27] We know these angels commute because they periodically report to God in heaven about the quality of their service on earth.[28]

29

Will we meet these angels in heaven? Abraham, Isaiah, and John talked to angels,[29] and there is every reason to believe that we too will talk to the angels when we meet them in heaven. But why doesn't God allow us to talk to our guardian angels now? On rare occasions He does, but usually our guardians are required to keep their presence secret from us so we won't be tempted to worship them. The Apostle John attempted to worship an angel during his vision of future events, but the angel at whose feet John fell had to remind the Apostle that angels are basically only servants of God, just as believers on earth are.[30]

There is a distinct possibility that some of the "gods" of ancient Greek and Roman mythology were in reality fallen angels from heaven masquerading as gods from outer space. The "beneficent gods" of Von Daniken's *Chariots of the Gods* may well have been fallen angels who gave advanced scientific knowledge to certain peoples of earth in exchange for their worship. It is a fact that almost every "enlightened society" mentioned in Von Daniken's *Chariots of the Gods* ended up worshiping the beings who had given them so much free information. Unlike Satan, who had to inhabit an animal in order to tempt Eve, these sinful masqueraders apparently appeared to people in their angelic bodies, thereby lending additional credibility to their phony claim of being beneficent gods from outer space. It is apparently these fiendishly clever deceivers who are right now confined in "eternal bonds under darkness for the judgment of the great day."[31]

But in heaven we'll be talking to *good* angels—servants of God who have been guarding us in marvelous ways during our entire lives on earth. When we get to heaven we'll spend hours talking to the angels who have been assigned to watch over us on earth. What stories they'll tell—of protected babies and guarded teenagers, of cared-for adults and sheltered invalids! We'll marvel at the preserving power of God during hundreds of dangers that we never even knew existed! Only then will we know the full meaning of the words, "He will give His angels charge concerning you, to guard you in all your ways."[32] Only then will we fully understand the role of angels as "ministering spirits sent out to render service for the sake of those who will inherit salvation."[33]

Good, Better, Best

But what if we die before the Rapture? Are all these wonderful things true of heaven right now? We believe they are, with only one important exception. In general, being in heaven right now is "far better" than being on earth.[34] (When Paul used the expression "far better" he knew what he was talking about, for it was probably he who was temporarily caught up to heaven, as described in 2 Corinthians 12:1-4.) But in one sense heaven before the Rapture is incomplete, because even the saints in heaven today are waiting for the resurrection of their earthly bodies at the time of the Rapture.[35] (God will resurrect our earthly bodies to prove to the watching universe that Christ's sacrifice at Calvary fully conquered the curse of physical death, as explained in 1 Corinthians 15:53-57.)

If the saints in heaven before the Rapture do not yet have their resurrection bodies, in what form do they exist? Are they just floating spirits? Some people think so, but the Bible seems to indicate that believers who die before the Rapture receive special heavenly bodies which serve them well until the Rapture and resurrection. When Saul consulted the witch of Endor, he ended up *seeing* the physical form of deceased Samuel.[36] When Peter, James, and John accompanied Christ to the Mount of Transfiguration, they *saw* Moses and Elijah talking with Jesus.[37] When the rich man in hades looked across that great gulf into paradise, he *saw* Abraham, with Lazarus in his bosom.[38] Second Corinthians 5:1-4 tells us, "For we know that if the earthly tent which is our house is torn down [referring to physical death for believers], we have a building from God, a house not made with hands [our new heavenly body], eternal in the heavens. For indeed in this house [our earthly body] we groan, longing to be clothed with our dwelling from heaven [our heavenly body], inasmuch as we, having put it on, shall not be found naked [disembodied]. For indeed while we are in this tent we groan, being burdened, because we do not want to be unclothed [disembodied] but to be clothed, in order that what is mortal may be swallowed up by life."

Yes, believers who die before the Rapture do have beautiful bodies in heaven, but these are not identical to the glorious new bodies which we will get at the time of the Rapture and resurrection. For one thing, our resurrection bodies will shine with the glowing beauty of Christ's own resurrection body.[39] For another thing, our beautiful new resurrection bodies will be suited not only for *heaven*, but for *earth* as well. Remember that Christ walked the dusty roads of Palestine in His resurrection body before He ascended to heaven.[40] The reason we will need a *dual-purpose* body is to commute between heaven and earth in the Millennium, since during Christ's thousand-year reign we'll be sharing His earthly rulership with Him if we've served Him well in the here-and-now.[41] Our resurrection bodies will have the wonderful capacity of living beautifully both in heaven above and on earth below.

The three possible bodies for a believer can be simply explained in this way:

Good—our present earthly body, corrupted by sin but still retaining a little of the original "image of God."[42]

Better—our heavenly body before the time of the Rapture and resurrection, suitable for heaven only.[43]

Best—our resurrection body, glorious in holiness and suitable for both heaven and earth.[44]

That's why even the saints in heaven are eagerly awaiting Christ's shout in the clouds!

Pass in Review

In John 10:27-30 Jesus said, "My sheep hear My voice, and I know them and they follow Me; and

I give eternal life to them, and they shall never perish, and no one shall snatch them out of My hand. My Father, who has given them to Me, is greater than all, and no one is able to snatch them out of the Father's hand. I and the Father are one." When we come to Jesus for salvation we do not come on the basis of our own good works. As Paul wrote in Ephesians 2:8, 9, "For by grace you have been saved through faith, and that not of yourselves; it is the gift of God, not as a result of works, that no one should boast." The security of our eternal salvation rests entirely on Christ's perfect finished work at the Cross of Calvary. Once we've acknowledged our own helplessness and received Christ as the sole Savior from our sin and its punishment, there's not another thing we can do to assure our eternal destiny in heaven.

But pleasing our Lord in our day-to-day lives here on earth is another matter entirely. Though in the final analysis our strength for daily Christian living comes entirely from Christ and the Holy Spirit, we obviously have some say in how fully we yield ourselves to the available power of God.[45] Again, this is not a question of where we will spend eternity, but a question of fellowship *within the family of God*.[46] When we ignore the Lord in our daily Christian lives, we grieve Him and jeopardize the happiness of our fellowship with Him, but when we confess our sins as Christians, the Lord is "faithful and righteous to forgive us our sins and to cleanse us from all unrighteousness."[47] If we persist in wandering from the Lord, even though we are part of God's family, God will correct us (but not punish us) in some way that effectively restores us to full, happy fellowship within the family.[48] The Bible makes it plain that no Christian is so consistently spiritual that he never needs to be corrected by God, for "what son is there whom his father does not discipline?"[49]

Sometime shortly after we get raptured to heaven, all of us in heaven will "pass in review" at the Judgment Seat of Christ.[50] Again, this is not to question whether we belong in heaven, but to review how faithfully we've served the Lord during our lifetime on earth.

Gems or Junk?

Second Corinthians 5:10 tells us, "For we must all appear before the judgment seat of Christ, that each one may be recompensed for his deeds in the body, according to what he has done, whether good or bad." The risk in this verse is not that we will be deported from heaven to hell, but that we will be personally ashamed and grieved when Christ reviews our earthly lives in the light of His perfect standards. First Corinthians 3:11-15 elaborates on this great day of review in heaven: "For no man can lay a foundation other than the one which is laid, which is Jesus Christ. Now if any man builds upon the foundation with gold, silver, precious stones, wood, hay, straw, each man's work will become evident, for the day will show it, because it is to be revealed with fire. And the fire itself will test the quality of each man's work. If any man's work which he has built upon it remains, he shall receive a reward. If any man's work is burned up, he shall suffer loss, but he himself shall be saved, yet so as through fire."

We have the option of accumulating a lifetime's worth of precious gems or of straw. But we need to know that the quality of our earthly activities will become a matter of public record after we get to heaven. Not that we'll be looking around with accusing eyes at someone else's failures—each one of us will have enough failures of his own! Yet most of us will receive at least some reward from the gracious God of heaven, and even the least faithful Christian will still remain saved, even if almost all his earthly works are burned up as valueless.[51]

But our goal shouldn't be to make it to heaven in spite of a wasted life on earth, but to "press on toward the goal for the prize of the upward call of God in Christ Jesus."[52] Since the rewards given at the Judgment Seat of Christ will last forever, what a tragedy it would be to arrive at that great day with nothing to be rewarded for! Two of the types of rewards to be given at the Judgment Seat of Christ include eternal crowns of glory and rulership over cities of the millennial earth.[53] Later in this book we will be studying the joys of these rewards in greater detail.

Beast or Feast?

One of the friendliest things you can do for a person is to invite him home for dinner. A dinner invitation is an almost-sure sign of cordial feelings; rarely do alienated people voluntarily eat together.

One of the happiest of all occasions for a fellowship feast is a wedding dinner. Here the bride and groom share their nuptial joys with dozens or hundreds of invited guests. And this is the kind of happy celebration that awaits us in heaven.

Sometime within the seven-year period from the Rapture to Christ's return to earth will be a great feast of heaven called the Marriage Supper of the Lamb: "Let us rejoice and be glad and give the glory to Him, for the marriage of the Lamb has come, and His bride has made herself ready.... Blessed are those who are invited to the marriage supper of the Lamb."[54]

Our "marriage" to Christ will take place at the time of the Rapture, and our wedding guests will include all the redeemed hosts of heaven. There will undoubtedly be literal eating and drinking at that great celebration supper, for Christ Himself ate more than one fellowship meal with his earthly disciples after His own resurrection.[55] A magnificent toast will be offered at that feast of heaven, but the toast won't be made to any dignified saint, not even the Apostle Paul. The toast will be made to the Bridegroom Himself, the Lord Jesus Christ, Savior of man and joy of heaven. There will be happy conversation among the guests and even wholesome laughter, for sinless happiness and laughter are within the perfect will of God.[56] This feast will be no ethereal, nebulous affair, but a real, tangible event with actual tables, food, and people. It will put to shame the most lavish V.I.P. banquet we've ever enjoyed on earth.

But on the earth at this very time will be a

starkly tragic contrast. By now the "Beast," Satan's tribulation Antichrist, will have gained control of most of the world. By now every person on earth will be compelled to have his hand or forehead indelibly identified with the mark of the Beast if he wishes to buy or sell anything at all—food included.[57] Most of earth's citizens will reluctantly bow to the will of the Beast, but the believers saved on earth after the Rapture will refuse to bow to anyone but Christ Himself,[58] and these people will find themselves slowly starving to death.

On the other hand, the people who bow to the will of the Beast will become subject to the eternal wrath of God for denying the sole supremacy of the Creator and Sustainer of the universe.[59] For both believers and unbelievers on earth, the Tribulation will be a time of unprecedented horror. How much better to receive Christ right now and be sure that we'll be present at that coming feast of heaven!

Chapter 4

I SEE, I SEE

Now we see in a mirror dimly, but then face-to-face; now I know in part, but then I shall know fully, just as I also have been fully known.

—1 Corinthians 13:12

The lights burned late in building F as Dr. Johnson struggled with the riddle of the test tubes. Why would the answer not come? For years he had been exploring the biological mystery of cancer, but still nature kept its secret from the pursuit of the searching scientist. Sometimes it hardly seemed worth continuing the effort.

Dr. Johnson's dilemma is as old as Adam and Eve. At first the happy couple had been secure in their God-given knowledge of their Edenic environment, but when Satan offered his bait of "knowledge as the gods," Eve quickly yielded to his ploy, and Adam soon followed.[1] But now their only increased knowledge was that of their own sinfulness in the sight of the Creator![2] From now on, true knowledge about the universe around them would be gained only by struggle and toil.[3]

The Knowledge of God

Fortunately for Adam and Eve, knowledge about God Himself was restored to them within hours after they had sinned.[4] All through the long story of human history God has been revealing His holiness and love to man in progressively greater detail, first in oral form, then in written form, and finally in the most glorious form of all—Jesus, the divine-human Savior of mankind.[5] First in the manger, then on the Cross and in the empty tomb, and finally in His triumphant return at the end of the Tribulation, the Lord Jesus Christ is the ultimate expression of the nature of God Himself.[6] Now that we have a completed Bible, plus the Holy Spirit to help us understand this Bible, we are able to enjoy the richest understanding of spiritual truth in all of human history up to this point.[7]

Yet we sense that there is still more to learn about God and angels and men. Somehow we sense that we're exploring the tip of an infinite iceberg, that the grandeur of God is too great to be grasped in the bustle of suburban living. We agree with Paul when he said, "Now we see in a mirror dimly, but then face-to-face; now I know in part, but then I shall know fully, just as I also have been fully known."[8]

Perfect Vision

What will knowledge in heaven be like? God, of course, knows everything already, and over the centuries the angels have accumulated an immense body of knowledge of both sacred and "secular" truths. (But of course angels will never have the infinite knowledge that God Himself has.) Abraham, Moses, and all the other long-term residents of heaven have by now accumulated almost as much knowledge as the angels (and in the issue of personal salvation, even more knowledge),[9] but how about the newcomers to heaven at the time of the Rapture? What will our heavenly enlightenment be like? Will we suddenly know everything there is to know about God and the universe, or will our education be progressive?

Certain information in heaven, such as the date of Christ's return to earth, is known only to God the Father Himself.[10] Though our knowledge in heaven will be immense, it can never be completely infinite, since only God can know everything in the universe.[11] Then what is the meaning of the words, "Now I know in part, but then I shall know fully, just as I also have been fully known?"[12] We believe these words mean that our knowledge in heaven will be perfect in *quality*, though not necessarily in *quantity*. In other words, whatever we know we will understand flawlessly, free from any distortion of meaning. This is the sense in which we will know fully, even as we have been fully known by God Himself. Though our knowledge of God and ourselves will take a quantum leap forward when we reach heaven, there will continue to be things for us to learn throughout the ages of eternity. For example, on at least one occasion during the course of the Tribulation, the believers in heaven will ask Christ an urgent question about the time-schedule of the Tribulation period.[13]

Bible Class Forever

But will all our information come directly from

Christ Himself? In Psalm 119, that great chapter on the virtues of God's written Scriptures, we read, "Forever, O Lord, Thy Word is settled in heaven" (verse 89). Isaiah 40:8 tells us, "The grass withers, the flower fades, but the Word of our God stands forever." God will never do away with His written Scriptures, not even in heaven. Everything that Jesus tells us in heaven will be corroborated by the written Word of God, and our eternal education will come from *two* basic sources—the Bible as the eternal *written* Word of God, and Jesus Himself as the eternal *personal* Word of God. Remember that Christ quoted often from the Bible when He taught people here on earth.[14]

But which translation will we use in heaven? The New Testament even suggests an answer to this question, for the New Testament writers quoted from the Septuagint, the then-popular Greek translation of the Old Testament, whenever this version was accurate enough to get the Old Testament message across. But wherever the Septuagint lacked accuracy, the New Testament writers quoted directly from the ancient Hebrew text of the Old Testament. We believe that most of us will use the Bible in at least two forms when we get to heaven: we will still quote and cherish whatever translation we have come to love during our learning years on earth, but we will also study the richness of the original Hebrew and Greek Scriptures. With our increased capacity for learning, all of us will be able to learn Hebrew and Greek with no great agony of mind, and every one of us will be multilingual in heaven. In addition, we will have a totally flawless text of Scripture written in the original languages—no more arguments about texts and versions!

Learning from Paul?

Will we also learn from each other in heaven? We can't give a dogmatic answer to this question, but it is a fact that Abraham (rather than God or an angel) answered the questions of the rich man in hades.[15] And Samuel himself (rather than God or an angel) delivered the warning message from heaven to disobedient King Saul.[16] And heavenly beings (rather than God Himself) revealed certain parts of the Book of Revelation to John the Apostle on the Island of Patmos.[17]

It is easy to imagine questioning Paul about some of the difficult concepts which he wrote under the guidance of the Holy Spirit. And how about the psalms of David? Won't it be great to review the personal story that went into the making of each inspired psalm? And how about the history of the ancient martyrs? Hebrews 11:32 tells us that the complete story of God's heroes of faith was too lengthy to put into print. All the millions of God's people who have ever lived, from the dawn of history to the time of the Rapture, will have fascinating stories to tell about the keeping power of God, and you too will have your opportunity to testify about the daily grace of God! Christian fellowship, testimony, and teaching will be alive and well in heaven!

Then Sings My Soul

How about singing in heaven? What kinds of songs will we sing when we get there? In addition to the spoken chants of worship quoted in Revelation 4:11 and 5:12, 13, we will sing musical hymns of praise and adoration to the God of our salvation. The theme of one of the new songs we will sing is described for us in Revelation 5:9, 10: "Worthy art Thou to take the book and to break its seals, for Thou wast slain and didst purchase for God with Thy blood men from every tribe and tongue and people and nation, and Thou hast made them to be a kingdom and priests to our God, and they will reign upon the earth."

No doubt we will sing variations on this theme which are set to meter and rhyme:

> Every kindred, tongue, and nation,
> Worthy the Lamb!
> Join to sing the great salvation,
> Worthy the Lamb!
> Loud as mighty thunders roaring,
> Floods of mighty waters pouring,
> Prostrate at His feet adoring,
> Worthy the Lamb![18]

And we'll sing the old familiar hymns, too:

> Fairest Lord Jesus, Ruler of all nature,
> O Thou of God and man the Son,
> Thee will I cherish, Thee will I honor,
> Thou, my soul's glory, joy, and crown.

> Beautiful Savior, Lord of the nations,
> Son of God and Son of man,

  Glory and honor, praise, adoration
   Now and forevermore be Thine.[19]

If your favorite song brings glory to the Lord Jesus
Christ, in all probability you will someday sing it
with the massed choirs of the heavenly city! Now is
the time for us to build up a repertory of songs that
qualify for the eternal courts of heaven.

Better than Bach

  Will Revelation 5:9, 10 be the only new song
that we sing in heaven? We think not. We think the
Holy Spirit will inspire our transformed minds to
compose music that is better than Bach or Handel at
their best. Handel's *Messiah* is a great work of praise
to God, but it is only a prelude to the masterpieces
of musical worship that we will compose during the
ages of eternity.

  And there will be instrumental music, too.
Revelation 14:2 specifically mentions harps and har-
pists, but we're sure there will be other musical in-
struments in heaven as well. All of us who are
frustrated pianists, violinists, or trumpeters will for
the first time be able to worship God musically
without the humiliation of a departing audience!
Now for the first time we'll be able to provide a
beautiful and worshipful accompaniment to the
massed voices of praise to God. And the singers—
those of us who are afraid to be heard outside the
shower—all of us will be invited to sing in the eternal choir of heaven![20] Even the angels will listen to
the sweet voices of the resurrected saints.

Holy History

Nowadays the term "holy history" is often used sarcastically by certain skeptical critics of the Bible. But in heaven the words will have a pure and straightforward meaning, because then for the first time we will see all of world history interpreted from the viewpoint of God Himself. It's true that the Bible tells us right now what God thinks of the *general flow* of world history, but in that day we'll know all the *details* as well—all of God's workings in the founding and preservation of the United States of America, for example. Instead of being interpreted from a relativistic, humanistic viewpoint, the history of Western civilization will be seen from the factual perspective of God Himself. No more disputed dates, names, or places, either. Everything will fit into one vast, beautiful mosaic of the active and permissive will of God. Even the career of Satan and his angels will be unfolded to us fully and clearly for the first time. Nothing will be left to guesses or hypotheses.

And of course we'll study other subjects too—mathematics, biology, astronomy, geology—every field of knowledge that has eluded the full grasp of earth's finest researchers today. No longer will there be an artificial distinction between "sacred" and "secular" knowledge, for *all* knowledge will bring glory to God and benefit to the learner. Christians born in poverty and reared in ignorance will for the first time enjoy the glow of a fully enlightened mind. Uneducated believers from every era of world history will now become experts in engineering, theology, and music. No intellectual handicap of earth will be too great for the Lord of heaven to correct.

A Knowledge of Earth

Once we get to heaven, will we still be able to know what's happening on earth? This question has intrigued people for centuries, but few Christians have attempted to find a Biblical answer for it. Yet the Bible does provide some clear information on this issue. In 1 Samuel 28:15-19 the deceased prophet Samuel, speaking from heaven to disobedient King Saul, displayed an accurate and detailed knowledge of the events of Saul's kingdom. On at least two occasions during the coming Tribulation period, the believers who are in heaven will speak to God about events which are happening on the earth at that time.[21] Abraham, Moses, and Elijah also displayed surprising knowledge about events outside heaven itself.[22] This really shouldn't surprise us too much, since the earth will continue to be one of Christ's major theaters of operation in the universe, and since we as Christ's intimate companions will share all His concerns with Him.[23] Even a knowledge of hades itself will apparently be available to some or all believers in heaven.[24] (But of course no one from heaven will be able to *visit* the realm of the lost.)[25]

Our main concern about earth events will not be the color of dress which Mrs. Jones is wearing, but the will of God performed on earth, as well as man's response to God's perfect will and Satan's interference with it. The earthly events that will concern us in heaven will be the broad movements of the Christian faith—the conversion of people during the Tribulation, the persecution of the believers because of their loyalty to Christ, and the growing power of Satan and his human spokesmen.[26]

Christ Himself is watching our earthly actions from heaven right now, but not as some malevolent "Big Brother" gleefully waiting to condemn us. Instead, He watches us with a yearning heart, earnestly waiting for us to receive Him as our Savior and to follow Him every day as the Lord of our lives.

Chapter 5

WARRIOR FROM HEAVEN

The Lord Jesus shall be revealed from heaven with His mighty angels, in flaming fire taking vengeance on those who do not know God and do not obey the gospel of our Lord Jesus Christ.

—2 Thessalonians 1:7, 8 RKJV

Once a wealthy but generous farmer leased out his vineyard to willing renters. The farmer had planted the vineyard, walled the property, and provided the proper equipment for extracting wine from the grapes. All the tenants had to do was to farm the land, take their fair share of the profits, and return the remainder to the owner. When harvest-time came, the owner, who was in another country at the time, sent one of his trusted employees to audit the finances of the vineyard and to return with a fair share of the profits for the owner.

But by this time the tenants had gotten greedy and rebellious, so they physically assaulted the farmer's employee and sent him away empty-handed. Shocked, the farmer sent another employee, but he too was beaten and locked out of the premises. The farmer sent still another employee, but he was not just beaten, but savagely murdered. "Who can I send to straighten out this mess?" the farmer asked himself. "There's only one answer—I'll send my own son. Surely they'll respect the son of the owner."

So the wealthy farmer sent his only son thousands of miles to the leased vineyard. But when the violent men of the vineyard saw the owner's son approaching, they said to themselves, "Here comes the boss's only heir to his fortune. If we kill the son, maybe we'll be able to keep the vineyard for ourselves." So the brutal tenants murdered the farmer's only son and threw his body over the wall of the vineyard.

What would you do if you were the wealthy but generous farmer whose only son had just been murdered?

That's exactly what God the Father will do with the millions of people on earth who reject His only Son given at Calvary![1]

Gentle Jesus?

This parable is found in Matthew 21:33-42, Mark 12:1-11, and Luke 20:9-18, and it illustrates an important point about the nature of God the Father and the Lord Jesus Christ. We sometimes tend to think that "gentle Jesus" is so meek and humble He wouldn't hurt a fly. Though this is true of Jesus in a certain sense, it is tragically false in a still more important sense. It is true that while Jesus was on earth He endured untold humiliations without uttering a word of protest,[2] but it is also true that the coming King will have plenty to say and do to the enemies who have rejected Him.[3] God never intended that the humiliation of Christ should be permanent—it was enough that the Son of God should be scorned and rejected by the majority of the human race for the thirty-odd years that Christ was on the earth, compounded by nearly two thousand years of additional rejection since the time of His death and resurrection.[4] The day is coming, and perhaps sooner than we think, that this "gentle Jesus" will become the mighty Warrior from heaven, "in flaming fire taking vengeance on those who do not know God and do not obey the gospel of our Lord Jesus Christ."[5]

When is this day of vengeance and fire? It is the day when Christ comes back to earth as its King—the day His enemies are punished and His friends are rewarded at the very end of the seven-year Tribulation period. The punishment will be physical death and eternal condemnation, and the reward will be physical life in the Millennium followed by eternal life in God's new earth and universe (see *Guide to the New World* on page 140).

Prelude to Hell

But of course Christ's return to earth as King won't happen today—it will be preceded by "the day of vengeance of our God,"[6] those terrible future years of Tribulation horror that await everybody left behind at the Rapture. The Bible has plenty to say about this "time of Jacob's trouble,"[7] and here are two samples: "Then there will be a great tribulation, such as has not occurred since the beginning of the world until now, nor ever shall."[8] "And the kings of the earth and the great men and the commanders, and the rich and the strong and every slave and free man, hid themselves in the caves and among the rocks of the mountains, and they said to the mountains and to the rocks, 'Fall on us and hide us from the presence of Him who sits on the throne and from the wrath of the Lamb, for the great day of their wrath has come, and who is able to stand?' ''[9]

Those days of tribulation will be unprecedented in the history of the world. It is a fact that the number of earthquakes reported worldwide has been steadily increasing, but the killer quakes we're witnessing today will only be third-page news in the coming days of the Tribulation. In those days entire cities will fall from the quakes, and islands will disappear from the surface of the sea.[10] It's true that we're witnessing some tragic famines today, but in the days of the Tribulation millions of people will die in a matter of weeks because of worldwide famines followed by unchecked pestilences and attacks by hungry animals.[11] We think World War Two was a terrible bloodbath, and so it was, but in those coming days of God's judgment, not *2 percent* but *50 percent* of the entire earth's population will be destroyed during the course of the Tribulation period![12] And then, when Christ returns as the "Warrior from heaven" at the very end of the Tribulation period, *all* the remaining unbelievers will be destroyed and sent to hell.[13]

Satan's Phony Rapture

But the Tribulation won't begin with earthquakes and death. It will begin instead with the sudden and mysterious disappearance of millions of adults and children around the world. Panic will grip the world for several days, followed by an ominous foreboding of coming events. There will be various theories about this unprecedented disappearance, with the Rapture explanation being true and the other theories being false. One of the dominant false theories will be that of UFO kidnappings. Even now phony UFO kidnappings are beginning to crop up in various parts of America and the world, but in the days after the Rapture these "kidnappings" will proliferate enormously as part of Satan's overall plan to blunt the truth about the real Rapture and resurrection. (For convincing evidence that UFO's are demonic manifestations, see *UFO's: What on Earth Is Happening?* by Weldon and Levitt.)[14] Within days after the Rapture, every TV network in America will have presented this UFO theory plus several others as explanations for the stunning event that has just taken place.

Banks, finance companies, and other lending institutions will be lost in a nightmare of red tape because of the disappearance of millions of borrowers and lenders. Employment throughout the nation and the world will be severely disrupted as some of the most strategic employers and employees in the business world disappear without a trace. Government legislatures at the local, state, and federal level will be severely crippled by the sudden absence of some of their most respected members. Thousands of patients will disappear from hospitals, and hundreds of inmates will disappear from jails and prisons! The Rapture will truly become the mystery of the century.

Saved or Lost?

Since all the bona fide Christian preachers will be gone at the Rapture, how will anyone on earth be able to get saved after this event? We believe it will be by literature. Remember that millions of Bibles, books, and tracts exist in homes throughout the world today. It's true that many of these Bibles are dust-covered right now, but after the Rapture thousands upon thousands of terrified people will open these dusty Bibles in a desperate search for eternal life. And many thousands of both Jews and non-Jews will find eternal life in the pages of Holy Scripture.[15] These new believers won't technically be part of "the church" (since that name applies only to people saved between the apostolic Day of Pentecost and the event of the Rapture), but they will still be bona fide children of God. It is these new believers, especially the Jewish ones, who will end up enduring the venom of the Antichrist and the agonies of worldwide persecution.[16]

Satan's Antichrist

At first the persecution won't be severe. Because of the rapidly deteriorating moral condition of the world, people will be concerned mostly about political peace and national survival. With the restraining influence of the Holy Spirit gone,[17] all the depressing trends that we see developing in the United States and around the world today will explode into an avalanche of violence and anarchy. Our present-day rottenness will seem like a Sunday

school picnic when compared with the cesspool of
the Tribulation. As in the pre-Hitler days of Ger-
many, millions of citizens will cry out for someone—
anyone—to save the world from utter chaos.

And from the darkness will step a man—a scin-
tillating, charismatic man who grips the whole
world with his sincerity of purpose and competence
of style. Where will he come from, and what will his
name be? Only God knows for sure. Think of this for
a moment: because Satan lacks the power and
knowledge of God and cannot predict accurately
when the Tribulation will begin, he has had to
remain busy preparing potential antichrists from the
earliest days of church history! For example, most of
the early Christians thought that inhuman Caesar
Nero was the Antichrist, and in all probability Satan
hoped that he would be. But God had other plans.

And so it was down through all the centuries of
church history. At all times Satan has had to have
one or more Antichrist candidates waiting in the
wings, lest the Rapture come suddenly and find him
unprepared. That is why so many malevolent world
leaders have had names whose letters added up to
666 when combined in certain ways. (Depending on
which 666 formula is used, at any given moment
there are several hundred thousand men in the
world whose names add up to 666. It is from this
large pool of candidates that Satan has traditionally
chosen his "man of the moment.") There is no
doubt that Satan sincerely hoped and believed that
Adolf Hitler would fulfill all the Biblical prophecies
about the end-time Antichrist. But Satan was wrong,
and so were hundreds of well-meaning Bible

teachers. That is why it behooves us to be careful about speculations on the identity of the actual end-time Antichrist.

The Mark of the Beast

As the Tribulation progresses, conditions in the world will get worse and worse. The charismatic leader of peace will gradually get more and more dictatorial, and 3½ years after the signing of his masterfully crafted peace treaty between Israel and her hostile neighbors, the Antichrist will without warning void the treaty and present himself as God in Jerusalem's newly-built temple.[18] Horrified, the Jewish people and much of the rest of the world will rise up in protest against the dictatorship of this Jekyll-and-Hyde monster.

But it will be too late. By this time the Antichrist will be so firmly entrenched in the politics of the world that no resisting people could hope to survive as a nation. And so the citizens will bow with grudging hatred. To force worldwide subjection, the Antichrist will compel every citizen on earth to receive some kind of indelible 666 mark on his forehead or hand.[19] Because this mark will signify recognition of the Beast's claim to divinity, Christ's newly converted believers on earth will never be able to comply. Furious, the Antichrist will forbid all trade of any kind for unmarked citizens, and no true believer will be able to buy or sell anything—not even food for survival.[20] As in the terrible prewar days of Poland and Holland, citizen will help citizen in a vast underground network of survival. Many of

Christ's believers will be caught and punished with death, and the ranks of the martyrs will multiply every day of the week.[21]

And the earth itself will be pounded by the judgments of God. Giant asteroids will scream into land and sea, and the waves of the seas will respond to these gravitational disruptions by smashing the shorelines of the world with immense tidal waves.[22] All of the earth's green vegetation and one-third of its trees will be devastated by fire, and hundreds of mountain peaks will be jarred loose by colossal earthquakes.[23] Sun and moon will be darkened to a bloody glow, and the people will scream in fear at the terrors in earth and sky.[24]

For many people there will still be an opportunity to repent, yet most of them will gnaw their tongues in pain as they curse the God of heaven.[25] Not even this prelude to hell itself will change the minds of the masses left behind on darkened planet earth.

Warrior from Heaven

As the Tribulation draws to a close, the warring armies of Russia, China, and the Arab nations will converge for their final colossal slaughter in the Valley of Megiddo (Armageddon), north of Jerusalem.[26] The fragile alliance between Russia and Egypt will be broken forever as Russia plunders the wealth of the Egyptian alliance but is then buffeted by the resurgent Arab nations.[27] The real battle will be over the possession of Jerusalem, but the warring nations will never be able to seize their prey, for at exactly the right moment the skies of the world will light up with the brightness of Christ as He returns to earth to take over the world as its King of Righteousness.[28]

Every eye will see Him,[29] and the fear of Christ's enemies will be unspeakable as they finally realize that their time of just punishment has come. Blood will compete with water for space in the streams and ditches of the land of Palestine as the hellish armies of Armageddon are destroyed forever by Christ Himself.[30] The Antichrist (the Beast) and his False Prophet, along with all the false prophets of the Tribulation era, will be seized by Christ and sent to their long-overdue punishment in the lake of fire.[31]

Those are the days when the clever deceivers will cry out to Christ, "Lord, Lord, have we not prophesied in Your name, and in Your name cast out demons, and in Your name done many wonderful works?"[32] But Christ will reply to them, "I never knew you; depart from Me, you who work iniquity."[33] Those are the days when Christ Himself will decide between the "sheep" and the "goats," and only Christ's believing sheep will enter His millennial kingdom on earth.[34]

Of Men and Angels

When Christ comes down from heaven at the end of the Tribulation period, He will be accompanied by millions of saints and angels. Christ would not have to share this honor with anyone, since He alone bore the agony of sin's penalty at

Calvary, but in His grace He has promised that all of us who honor Him on earth will in turn be honored at His public conquest of the world: "The Lord Jesus shall be revealed from heaven with His mighty angels in flaming fire . . . when He comes to be glorified in His saints on that day and to be marveled at among all who have believed (2 Thessalonians 1:7, 10). Jude 14, 15 adds, "Behold, the Lord comes with ten thousands of His saints to execute judgment upon all,"[35] and Revelation 19:14 describes our participation this way: "The armies which are in heaven, clothed in fine linen, white and clean, were following Him on white horses." The massed armies of heaven will outnumber all the military might assembled in the Valley of Armageddon! Yet it seems that the military might of Christ alone will be all that is necessary to crush forever the rebellious forces of earth, for it is "the sword of Christ's mouth" that strikes down the hostile nations in one fell swoop of judgment.[36]

The Back of the Bus?

But not every Christian will be in front of Christ's returning armies from heaven. Only those believers who have served Christ well in the here-and-now will receive positions near the white-horse Rider Himself: "For whoever is ashamed of Me and My words in this adulterous and sinful generation, the Son of man will also be ashamed of him when He comes in the glory of His Father with the holy angels."[37] If we are ashamed of Christ in our present life on earth, He will be ashamed of us when

He comes to claim the earth for Himself. We will still be saved, for 1 Corinthians 3:15 assures us, "If any man's work is burned up he shall suffer loss, but he himself shall be saved, yet so as through fire." If we're lazy Christians right now, we'll still make it to heaven by death or the Rapture, and we'll even make it back to earth at Christ's glorious second coming, but we'll be "at the back of the bus" as far as our position in His heavenly army is concerned.

With Isaac Watts each one of us should be willing to say,

> When I survey the wondrous Cross
>   on which the Prince of Glory died,
> My richest gain I count but loss,
>   and pour contempt on all my pride.

> Were the whole realm of nature mine,
>   that were an offering far too small;
> Love so amazing, so divine,
>   demands my heart, my life, my all.

Chapter 6

KING OF THE WORLD

*Give the King Thy judgments, O God, and Thy
righteousness to the King's son. . . . He shall
have dominion from sea to sea, and from the river
to the ends of the earth.*

—Psalm 72:1, 8 RKJV

The crowd is hushed as the conductor lifts his
baton in the Great Hall of Jerusalem. For another
moment all is silent, then twenty thousand voices
burst forth in a thunder of praise:

> O Lord my God, when I in awesome wonder
> Consider all the worlds Thy hands have
> made,
> I see the stars, I hear the rolling thunder,
> Thy power throughout the universe
> displayed—

Eighty thousand voices join in from the audience,

> Then sings my soul, my Savior-God to Thee,
> How great Thou art, how great Thou art!
> Then sings my soul, my Savior-God to Thee,
> How great Thou art, how great Thou art![1]

It is the annual Festival of Praise in Jerusalem, and
the King of the world, the Lord Jesus Christ, is once

again being honored by citizens from all over the world. Russians, Americans, Venezuelans, and Africans join the local Jewish singers in a thundering crescendo of worship to the God of the universe and the Savior of men. All around the world millions of redeemed citizens are watching the event on TV and are singing along with worshipful hearts. 2025 is the year, and the setting is the millennial kingdom of Christ on earth. The horrors of the Tribulation are long past now, and the tranquility of Christ's kingdom rule has been well-established.

King Adam

But why an earthly rulership for Christ at all? Why couldn't God just destroy the whole world after the battle of Armageddon and take all His believers permanently to heaven? Though some people think this is just what God will do, the Bible provides a very powerful reason why Christ *must* rule as King over this very planet earth.

When God created Adam and Eve He told them, "Be fruitful and multiply, and fill the earth and subdue it, and rule over the fish of the sea and over the birds of the sky and over every living thing that moves on the earth."[2] In other words, Adam and Eve were to be king and queen over the perfect earth which God had created. Psalm 8 describes the exalted position—only a little lower than the angels themselves—which God originally gave to Adam and Eve.

But as the Bible clearly teaches, the deliberate disobedience of these first two people plunged both themselves and their earthly environment into the agelong curse of sin.[3] As Romans 8:22 puts it, "We know that the whole creation groans and suffers the pains of childbirth together until now."

King Jesus

Will this groaning world ever be liberated from its curse of sin, or will it just be annihilated in favor of some better place in the sky? The Bible tells us that God's original plan for a perfect physical world will be gloriously vindicated at the second coming of Christ. As Psalm 8 and Romans 5:15-21 point out, Jesus Christ through His sacrificial death at Calvary has become the "second Adam," fully capable of undoing all the suffering caused by the first Adam.[4] The original Adam could have been the permanent king of the earth, but because of his rebellion against God he lost not only his earthly kingship but also his own physical immortality. The Lord Jesus Christ, on the other hand, has proved Himself fully qualified to be the King of the world and completely capable of granting both physical and spiritual immortality to everyone who puts his trust in Him. That is why Christ will someday become the unchallenged Ruler of this physical planet earth:

> Give the King Thy judgments, O God, and Thy righteousness to the King's son. May He judge Thy people with righteousness, and Thine afflicted with justice. Let the mountains bring peace to the people, and the hills in righteousness. May He vindicate the afflicted of the people, save the children of the needy, and crush the oppressor.

Let them fear Thee while the sun endures and as long as the moon, throughout all generations. May He come down like rain upon the mown grass, like showers that water the earth. In His days may the righteous flourish, and abundance of peace till the moon is no more.

May He also rule from sea to sea and from the River to the ends of the earth. Let the nomads of the desert bow before Him, and His enemies lick the dust. Let the kings of Tarshish and of the islands bring presents, the kings of Sheba and Seba offer gifts, and let all kings bow down before Him, all nations serve Him.[5]

The duration of this kingdom—1000 years—is mentioned six times in Revelation 20, and here is one of those mentions:

Blessed and holy is the one who has a part in the first resurrection; over these the second death has no power, but they will be priests of God and of Christ and will reign with Him for a thousand years.[6]

O Worship the King

For the first time in over four thousand years (since Noah and his family), the entire world population will worship the one true God of heaven and the one true Redeemer of men.[7] No more slander or blasphemy against the holy Son of God—every throat in every continent of the world will shout the praises of the noble King of the earth. In those days dozens of our favorite Scripture verses will take on their richest meanings as we "give to the Lord the glory due His name."[8]

We'll exclaim, "Thy kingdom come, Thy will be done in earth, as it is in heaven."[9] "Lift up your heads, O ye gates, even lift them up, ye everlasting doors, and the King of glory shall come in. Who is this King of glory? The Lord of hosts—He is the King of glory."[10] "Give unto the Lord, O ye mighty ones, give unto the Lord glory and strength; give unto the Lord the glory due unto His name. Worship the Lord in the beauty of holiness."[11] "Thou art fairer than the children of men; grace is poured into Thy lips. Therefore God hath blessed Thee forever. . . . Thy throne, O God, is forever and ever; the scepter of Thy kingdom is a right scepter . . . . I will make Thy name to be remembered in all generations; therefore shall the people praise Thee forever and ever."[12] "Great is the Lord and greatly to be praised in the city of our God, in the mountain of His holiness. Beautiful for situation, the joy of the whole earth, is Mount Zion on the sides of the north, the city of the great King."[13] "Praise waiteth for Thee, O God, in Zion, and unto Thee shall the vow be performed."[14] "Not unto us, O Lord, not unto us, but unto Thy name give glory, for Thy mercy and for Thy truth's sake."[15] Those are the days when all of us will sing,

> Jesus shall reign where'er the sun
>   doth his successive journeys run;
> His kingdom spread from shore to shore,
>   till moons shall wax and wane no more.

From north to south the princes meet
to pay their homage at His feet;
His name like sweet perfume shall rise
with every morning sacrifice.[16]

Those are days when Psalm 145 will thrill us as never before:

I will extol Thee, my God, O King, and I will bless Thy name forever and ever. Every day will I bless Thee, and I will praise Thy name forever and ever. Great is the Lord and greatly to be praised, and His greatness is unsearchable. One generation shall praise Thy works to another, and shall declare Thy mighty acts. I will speak of the glorious honor of Thy majesty and of Thy wondrous works . . . . All Thy works shall praise Thee, O Lord, and Thy saints shall bless Thee. They shall speak of the glory of Thy kingdom and talk of Thy power, to make known to the sons of men His mighty acts and the glorious majesty of His kingdom. Thy kingdom is an everlasting kingdom, and Thy dominion endureth throughout all generations.[17]

Temple Magnificent

High on a hill overlooking the beautiful new city of Jerusalem will glisten the magnificent new millennial Temple.[18] Down through the centuries of Palestine's stormy history, four temples of worship will have come and gone, but this fifth and final Temple will eclipse all the previous four, since it will endure for the entire thousand years of the Millennium and will give way only to the personal presence of the triune God Himself in the far-distant renovation of earth and sky. Never before will any temple of worship have commanded the attention of so many people all over the world. Never before will the glory of God have been so universally recognized by the citizens of earth. Never before will so many people have traveled so far to pay their homage to the King of Kings and Lord of Lords.

Not just Jews in Palestine, but people from all over the world will visit Jerusalem at least once a year to pay their personal tribute to the Lord of the nations.[19] Unlike today's warped and forced efforts at ecumenism, in those days a pure, one-world religion will become a reality in the Person of our Lord Jesus Christ.[20] Not just Old Testament Jews and pre-Rapture Christians, but all surviving believers of the Tribulation era, whether Jewish or non-Jewish, will worship Christ as their Savior and Lord every day of the year.

Remember Me

Beginning with the very first animal sacrificed by God in the Garden of Eden,[21] and continuing down through the centuries of human history to the death of Christ at Calvary, the blood of animals has been shed as an unforgettable picture of Christ's lifeblood poured out for our sins on the Cross of Calvary.[22] After Christ died and rose again, however, God decreed that the animal sacrifices should stop, so that all humanity would know that the symbolism of animal sacrifice had given way to the reality of Christ's perfectly completed sacrifice for sins.[23] And this has been the will of God from the day of Christ's resurrection to the first day of the Millennium to come.

Yet we do symbolize Christ's sacrificial death in another way: we break the bread and drink the wine in remembrance of the death of our Savior.[24] In other words, we do not look *forward* to some suffering Messiah still to come; instead, we look *backward* to a triumphant Redeemer who has not only died for our sins but has risen again and gone back to heaven to intercede daily on our behalf.

For the nonresurrected people of the Millennium (that is, those people on earth who will get saved after the Rapture and will manage to survive the horrors of the Tribulation), there will also be a recurring memorial which portrays the perfectly finished sacrifice of Christ at Calvary. What is this memorial? The sacrifice of animals in a definitely prescribed temple ceremony. The sacrifices will be somewhat similar to the Old Testament Jewish procedures in some respects, but in other ways the memorial sacrifices of the Millennium will be strikingly different. For details of the similarities and differences, compare Ezekiel 43:18 – 46:24 with Leviticus chapters 1 – 7. The important thing to remember is that in those days no one will misunderstand the meaning of the sacrifices; everyone will realize that the blood of the animals pictures a perfectly completed work of salvation by the Lord Jesus Christ Himself.

Oceans of Knowledge

"The earth will be full of the knowledge of the

Lord as the waters cover the sea," wrote Isaiah of the coming Millennium.[25] In those days everyone will know not just the names and the order of the books of the Bible, but everything *in* those books as well! The Bible memory programs will be unprecedented in the history of the world, and everyone will become an expert in Biblical theology. All those knotty interpretive problems of Scripture will be understood perfectly, not just in heaven but on earth as well. No more "contradictions in the Bible" or "synoptic problem" in the Gospels. No more quarrels over Genesis 6, Romans 6, or Hebrews 6, and no more battles over "a-mil," "post-mil," or "pre-mil" views of prophecy! Pre-, mid-, and post-tribulationists will long since have settled their differences in the light of Scripture, and even the Calvinists and Arminians will live in enlightened peace!

Many new Bible commentaries will be written, and every one of them will agree both with each other and with the Bible itself. Every new song will be completely Scriptural, even the ones written for the children in Sunday school! Every publisher of sacred literature will offer a selection of books that is 100 percent approved by Christ Himself, and every Christian radio and TV station will have reached the pinnacle of sacred and technical perfection. Even the daily newspapers will give glory to God and blessing to the people!

Farewell to Heresy

During the Millennium there will be no such

thing as heresy; every false view will long since have been exposed and corrected in the light of Scripture. No more direct or indirect attacks on the deity of Christ, the inspiration of Scripture, or the creatorial power of God. All arguments over whether Christ is the Creator-King or merely another creature will be put to rest forever, for there He will stand as the King to be adored and obeyed. All the debates about the truthfulness of Scripture will be nothing but museum relics, since the fulfilled Word of God will be witnessed every day by the teeming millions of earth's people.

People will marvel that the theory of evolution could ever have flourished in a past society that considered itself enlightened. The humanism and relativism that are sweeping our twentieth-century colleges and universities will be exposed as a cruel and demonic hoax, and the college students will instead revel in the liberty of God's eternal standards. Situation ethics will finally be seen for what it really is—an unloving, shortsighted philosophy that grabs whatever it can for the fun of the moment. Instead the millennial citizens will worship and work together in true Christian love, doing the will of God as correctly interpreted in the Bible.

Christian Ed for Everyone

In those days all education will be Christian. There will be no line of demarcation between "secular" and "sacred," for *all* knowledge will bring glory to God. Instead of grasping after nonexistent "missing links," people will learn God's exquisitely perfect purpose behind the creation of each plant and animal. Instead of theorizing on how this primate evolved from that lower mammal, your tour guide at the zoo will describe God's incredibly sophisticated design that went into the creation of each particular animal. People will study mathematics, astronomy, and physics not just for the bare facts of the subject, but to see how each area of science glorifies the God of creation.

There may continue to be planetary flights and space probes, but not for the purpose of finding some evolutionary origin of the universe, since by this time the Originator of the universe will be well-known to everybody in the world. World history will no longer be warped and twisted by biased writers, for the new history texts will show how things really happened and will interpret these events in the light of God's Biblical standards. Now for the first time the people of the world will clearly understand God's magnificent plan for the universe from eternity past to eternity future. Now for the first time the human race at large will understand its rightful role within the perfect will of God.

All of us can come within that perfect will of God for the universe right now, and the requirement is not difficult. All we need to do is to believe and receive God's good gift of eternal life offered to us in the Person of the Lord Jesus Christ. In a personal act of faith and commitment we need to turn ourselves over to the Lord Jesus Christ and begin our adventure of eternal life today.

Chapter 7

MY TEN CITIES

Well done, good servant. Because you have been faithful in a very little, have authority over ten cities.

—Luke 19:17 RKJV

On your marks! The voice of the official boomed through the stadium, and Eric positioned his feet perfectly in the starting blocks, as he had done a thousand times before. *Get set!* Eric lifted his body, every muscle tense for the starter's gun. *Bang!* Eight of the world's fastest men burst away from their starting blocks and streaked toward their goal 400 meters away. It was Eric's first Olympic competition, and he *must* win a medal, not just for himself but for the U.S.A. as well. His twelve years of grueling training *must* provide a victory for Eric today.

Two hundred meters were past now, and Eric was still in third place. That Russian! How could he be in first place? And that Jamaican, how could he be in second? Calling on every agonizing ounce of reserve in his body, Eric plunged toward the finish line in a desperate bid to overtake the Jamaican.

Here came the finish and the roar of the crowd. The Russian was first, but Eric was second! Defying all the predictions, Eric had outrun two of his American teammates plus five runners from foreign countries! The thrill of victory eclipsed the bittersweet agony of the race as Eric waited to receive his silver medal alongside the gold and bronze medals of the Russian and the Jamaican.

What a day of triumph! Without a doubt this was the finest hour of Eric's entire nineteen years. The twelve years of sweat and agony in the tracks of Michigan and California seemed as nothing when compared with the glory of this Olympic moment. How could any human being ever experience a greater glory than this?

Running the Race

"Everyone who competes in the games exercises self-control in all things," wrote Paul, and he added, "Run in such a way that you may win. . . . They . . . do it to receive a perishable wreath, but we an imperishable."[1] Eric's moment of glory was a great one, but at best its happy memory would linger with him for another sixty or seventy years, until death finally claimed Eric's old and worn-out body.

What a contrast to the Christian's race for Christ! Not just for sixty or seventy years, but for the ages of eternity itself we will enjoy the sweet fruits of victory. Not for our own glory, nor even for the honor of the U.S.A., but for the eternal glory of our Savior and Lord we "run with patience the race that is set before us."[2]

The agonies of the Christian race are not always easy to take, but we do have a racing Champion whose example we can follow: " . . . Jesus, the author and the perfecter of faith, who for the joy set before Him endured the cross, despising the shame, and has sat down at the right hand of the throne of God. For consider Him who has endured such hostility by sinners against Himself, so that you may not grow weary and lose heart. You have not yet resisted to the point of shedding blood in your striving against sin."[3] God alone knows the heartache and the suffering, the toil and the agony which each of us has faced, and God alone knows what our eternal reward will be. But we do know that if we have received Christ as our Savior and have lived even reasonably loyal lives for Him on earth, we will receive at least some eternal reward both in heaven and on the new earth: "If we suffer with Him we will also reign with Him. . . ."[4] "Thou hast made us kings and priests to our God, and we shall reign over the earth."[5]

From First to Last

"Many who are first shall be last, and the last first,"[6] said Jesus, and He knew what He was talking about. He saw then and He still sees now the hypocrisy that threatens to grip us all. How easy it is for us to put on a little show of goodness for our neighbors, our families, or our friends—and especially our church friends! How easy it is for us to admire that golden-tongued preacher or that silver-throated singer—or perhaps even to *be* that much-admired preacher or singer! How easy it is for us to "give alms to be seen of men"[7] or to put on a little charade of holiness for the benefit of the pastor or the congregation!

And it's just as easy for us to ignore that quiet widow who "prays without ceasing" in the privacy of her own home. Or how about that crippled lady who never gets around much, but who writes letters daily to missionaries all around the world? Or how about that retarded young man who always stands quietly in the back of the church, ignored by everybody except the pastor and a handful of sympathetic people? Could it be that this handicapped believer will receive a greater reward in heaven for his quiet devotion to Christ than we will for all our showy religious activity?[8] Only God can answer this question, and His answer will come at that future day of eternal rewards. The secret of pleasing God is neither frenzied Christian activity nor spiritual laziness; we please God most thoroughly by serving Christ and witnessing for Him in an attitude of continual, heartfelt worship.[9]

All the King's Men

We do not go to heaven because God owes us salvation, nor do we receive eternal crowns or cities because God owes us rewards for Christian service. Instead, we receive both salvation and rewards on the basis of God's gracious, giving nature. Paul wrote, "God, being rich in mercy, because of His great love with which He loved us, even when we were dead in our transgressions, made us alive together with Christ (by grace you have been saved) . . . in order that in the ages to come He might show the surpassing riches of His grace in kindness toward us in Christ Jesus. For by grace you have been saved through faith, and that not of yourselves; it is the gift of God, not as a result of works, that no one should boast."[10] Christ Himself said, "When you do all the things which are commanded you, say, 'We are unworthy slaves; we have done only that which we ought to have done.' "[11]

Yet the love of Christ is so great that He wants us to participate with Him in His eternal glories. When Christ comes back to earth at the end of the Tribulation, He will be accompanied by armies of saints from heaven,[12] and when He reigns over this world in His thousand-year Millennium, hundreds of thousands of believers from all eras of world history will share His rulership with Him.[13] Christ will, of course, be the ultimate Sovereign from whom all authority in the millennial world will flow, but there will also be many ranks of lesser officials to implement His rulership during this thousand-year period.[14] There will be resurrected rulers, for example, over groupings of five cities and ten cities: "Then the first servant came saying, 'Lord, Your pound has gained ten pounds.' And [Christ] said to him, 'Well done, good servant. Because you have been faithful in a very little, have authority over ten cities.' And the second servant came saying, 'Lord, Your pound has gained five pounds.' And He said likewise to him, 'You rule over five cities.' "[15]

This mayoral authority will be part of our future reward for serving Christ acceptably in our life on earth right now. At first the thought of ruling over five or ten cities may seem overwhelming to some of us, especially if we've done very little supervising during our earthly lives, but in our

resurrected bodies we'll be perfectly capable of ruling kindly and competently. We'll possess all the ex-
pertise in governmental rulership that we need,
since by this time we will have been thoroughly
trained in administrative skills by the Master Ad-
ministrator Himself. Very likely there will have been
orientation sessions in heaven during the seven
years of the earthly Tribulation period, so that as
soon as the Tribulation is over and the Millennium
begins, we will be able to undertake our rulership
duties with skill and confidence.

Harmony of Nations

Though the Jewish land and people will receive
special honor as the seat of government and worship
during the thousand years of the Millennium,[16] no
believer will be left out of God's perfect program for
paradise on earth. Even though the earth will have
been assaulted by earthquakes, asteroids, fires, and
perhaps nuclear warfare during the terrible days of
the Tribulation, the physical world itself will not
have been totally destroyed by these catastrophes.

There will be some important changes in the
world's climate, topography, and fertility, but the
basic geography of the millennial world will be
much the same as it is now. The distribution of
nations will be somewhat similar to our present
arrangement,[17] except that social injustices will be
rectified and all peoples of the world will live at
peace with each other and with God Himself. There
will continue to be distinct ethnic groups living in
the various continents of the world,[18] but instead of

bombing each other to gain additional land, people, or resources, the nations of the world will work together toward the common goal of glorifying God.[19]

Highways to Heaven

Paul tells us in 2 Corinthians 5:1, "We know that if the earthly tent which is our house is torn down, we have a building from God, a house not made with hands, eternal in the heavens." Peter tells us, "God . . . has caused us to be born again to a living hope through the resurrection of Jesus Christ from the dead, to obtain an inheritance which is imperishable and undefiled and will not fade away, reserved in heaven for you."[20] John the Apostle tells us in Revelation 5:9, 10, "They sang a new song, saying, 'Worthy art Thou to take the book and to break its seals, for Thou wast slain and didst purchase for God with Thy blood men from every tribe and tongue and people and nation, and Thou hast made them to be a kingdom and priests to our God, and they will reign upon the earth."

In other words, Peter and Paul tell us that *we have an eternal inheritance in heaven*, yet John tells us that *we will reign on the millennial earth*. How can these two distinct concepts be harmonized? We believe the answer is simple—resurrected believers will commute between heaven and earth during the Millennium, just as God's angels have been doing for thousands of years. The Bible promises us that our *eternal home is in heaven*, and it also promises us that *we will reign over the millennial world*, and the way both of these promises will be fulfilled is by daily commutation between heaven and earth, even as millions of businessmen commute to work daily in our present world.

During the day we will attend to our supervisory duties in some part of the world assigned to us by Christ Himself, and at night, when the nonresurrected earth people are sleeping, we will return to the heavenly city for eight or ten hours of celestial fellowship. Remember that one of the major reasons for which we will receive our resurrection bodies is to be able to function efficiently *either in heaven above or on earth below*. Whenever we are in heaven our bodies will glow with an intensity of resurrection glory which is proportional to our previous faithfulness to Christ (during our earthly lives before death or the Rapture),[21] but when we're attending to our earthly millennial duties our resurrection glory will be masked (even as Christ's was during His postresurrection earthly appearances),[22] so that the earth people won't be tempted to envy or venerate us. To them we'll look like ordinary people, even though they will probably realize that we actually possess resurrection bodies. (Earthly survivors of the Tribulation will live conventional lives on earth— marrying, bearing children, and living to a ripe old age.)[23]

Christ Himself may also commute between Jerusalem and the heavenly city, since His personal physical presence in Jerusalem will probably not be required during the sleeping hours of the night. If this is so, the resurrected believers who commute to the heavenly city during the night hours will fellowship not only with angels and other believers, but also with Christ Himself. Since the earth will probably continue to rotate on a 24-hour basis during the Millennium, the resurrected believers who rule over various parts of the globe in the daytime will commute to the heavenly city at night in staggered schedules. (For example, when it's daytime in Jerusalem it's nighttime in Japan.) The resurrected believers from various rulerships throughout the world will be able to visit Christ personally either in Jerusalem or in the heavenly city simply by using a rotating work schedule. And of course Christ will be free to physically visit His people in any part of the world anytime He wishes to.

Who Gets Hawaii?

How will the groupings of five or ten reward cities be distributed to the resurrected believers? Will there be a random drawing, or will there be a deliberate plan of God? We believe the cities will be assigned by Christ Himself, though with some freedom of choice on the part of the mayors-to-be, even as the ancient tribes of Israel were given some choice in the apportionment of the Promised Land.[24] In all probability the resurrected believers will be assigned those regions of earth in which they had lived before death or the Rapture. There will probably be no great rush to Hawaii, since all parts of the earth will now have a desirable climate. The greater thrill will be to rule over a redeemed and peaceful New York, Chicago, or Los Angeles! Since quite a few single-story buildings will probably have survived the Tribulation earthquakes, there may even continue to be a certain air of familiarity about some of our previous hometowns!

Better than Democracy

What form of government could possibly be better than democracy? This question has intrigued students of government for centuries. At one time the "beneficent monarchy" was thought to be the best form of government, but wise and beneficent monarchs have been so rare in the history of the world that political scientists have all but written off this form of government as an unattainable pipedream. In its absence, most of us would agree that the American form of democracy has served us well during the comparatively short history of the United States of America.

Yet democracy has its weak points too, and one of these is that there is no single force to write, execute, and enforce the laws of the land with justice. In certain parts of the country, poverty-stricken people are fined or even jailed for petty violations of poorly written laws, while in the big cities of America hundreds of major crimes go unsolved and unpunished every week of the year. The poor, the elderly, and the oppressed cry out for relief and protection from violent criminals, but no part of our government seems able to answer their pleas. We have learned to await with dread the FBI's yearly release of crime statistics, knowing that our worst fears of criminal violence will once again have been confirmed.

Not so in the Millennium. There for the first time in world history the full potential of the monarchical form of government will be realized. There for the first time a truly beneficent Monarch will rule over the world with perfect justice and love.[25] "Democracy was good in its time," the historians will write, "but Christ's theocracy is obviously superior in every respect. The nations are living in peace, the people are well supplied with every legitimate need, the employees are satisfied with their jobs, and the employers seem to genuinely care about the needs of the people. Educational standards are eclipsing anything in previous world history, and the purity of world worship could hardly have been imagined by any premillennial generation."

As Psalm 72 puts it, "Give the King Thy judgments, O God, and Thy righteousness to the King's son. He will judge Thy people with righteousness, and Thine afflicted with justice. The mountains will bring peace to the people, and the hills in righteousness. He will vindicate the afflicted of the people, save the children of the needy, and crush the oppressor. They will fear Thee while the sun endures, and as long as the moon, throughout all generations. He will come down like rain upon the mown grass, like showers that water the earth. In His days the righteous will flourish, and abundance of peace till the moon is no more. He will rule from sea to sea, and from the River to the ends of the earth . . . . He will deliver the needy when he cries for help, the afflicted also, and him who has no helper. He will have compassion on the poor and needy, and the lives of the needy He will save. He will rescue their life from oppression and violence, and their blood will be precious in His sight . . . . May His name endure forever; may His name increase as long as the sun shines, and let men bless themselves by Him. Let all nations call Him blessed."[26]

Chapter 8

NO MORE MEDICARE

No longer will babies die when only a few days old; no longer will men be considered old at 100; only sinners will die that young! . . . My people will live as long as trees and will long enjoy their hard-won gains.

—Isaiah 65:20, 22 TLB

"In that day the wolf and the lamb will lie down together, and the leopard and goats will be at peace. Calves and fat cattle will be safe among lions, and a little child shall lead them all. The cows will graze among bears; cubs and calves will lie down together, and lions will eat grass like the cows. Babies will crawl safely among poisonous snakes, and a little child who puts his hand in a nest of deadly adders will pull it out unharmed. Nothing will hurt or destroy in all my holy mountain, for as the waters fill the sea, so shall the earth be full of the knowledge of the Lord."[1]

A wishful pipedream? Not at all. The above words come straight from the Bible, and they refer to that beautiful future Millennium when men and animals will be at peace with God and each other.

People's Paradise

When Adam and Eve sinned in the Garden of Eden, they forfeited not only their own physical immortality, but also the life and liberty of the created world around them.² Plants and animals, fish and fowl would now share the agony of sin's curse for the long centuries until Christ returned to undo the sorrow of Adam's sin. "The whole creation groans and travails in pain together until now," Paul tells us in Romans 8:22, and he adds, "For the anxious longing of the creation waits eagerly for the revealing of the sons of God. For the creation was subjected to futility not of its own will but because of Him who subjected it, in hope that the creation itself also will be set fee from its slavery to corruption into the freedom of the glory of the children of God."³

It was necessary that the plants and animals should share the curse of Adam and Eve, so that lions, tigers, and jungle vines would not conquer cursed mankind and take over the world. But the day is coming when the curse on man, animals, plants, and soil will be lifted simultaneously, and the whole world will once again thrive the way God originally intended it to.⁴ How soon could this "people's paradise" come to pass? Within seven years of today, since that is the approximate length of time of the Tribulation following the Rapture. The "Great Society" envisioned by past U.S. presidents may be approaching sooner than we think, but it won't be by the genius of any elected official—it will be by the power of the Lord Jesus Christ Himself!

Young at 100

If Adam and Eve had not sinned, they would

have lived on forever in their physical bodies. But once they sinned, the decay of sin set in immediately, and the physical immortality of mankind became lost from the time of Adam until the coming Rapture and resurrection.[5] (We believe that Adam and Eve themselves were redeemed by the blood of Christ pictured in the animal which God sacrificed for them,[6] and that they will participate in the coming resurrection.) Even though Adam and Eve died *spiritually* the same day they sinned, we know they did not die *physically* at that same moment, since Adam lived physically another 930 years and even fathered a number of children.[7] But only three other men mentioned in the Bible (Methuselah, Jared, and Noah)[8] ever again lived as long as 930 years, for the vicious curse of sin was gradually corrupting the genes and chromosomes of the human race.[9]

After the flood of Noah the lifespan of mankind dropped still more sharply,[10] for the inbreeding of the race (among only the eight members of Noah and his family), coupled with the increased penetration of ultraviolet rays through the earth's atmosphere (caused by the loss of tremendous quantities of upper-atmosphere water vapor in the falling rain of the flood), deteriorated man's physical stamina still further. So rapid was this post-flood deterioration that, within a few generations after the flood, people were living only one-fourth as long as Adam and his immediate descendants.[11] (The progressively decreasing lifespans described in Genesis 5 and 11, coupled with the low ages of parenthood—as low as 29 years[12]—show that these lifespan specifications were based on actual years rather than on lunar months or some other short period.)

In the Millennium the human lifespan will once again be long, even longer than that of Adam and his descendants, for most earth people will survive the entire thousand years of the Millennium.[13] And of course *resurrected people*, the ones who commute from their home in heaven to their rulership duties on earth, won't have to worry about physical death at all, since guaranteed immortality is one of the features of their resurrection bodies.[14] Yet in the Millennium even *earth people*—the ones who get saved after the Rapture and manage to survive the horrors of the Tribulation—will live peaceful and fruitful lives "as long as trees."[15] Death will be a rarity and will be reserved mostly for the occasional violent criminal[16] (see Chapter 9).

Population Explosion

Because of the almost-complete removal of God's curse on living things during the Millennium,[17] human fertility among the nonresurrected earth people will prosper as never before (though of course *resurrected* believers will neither marry nor bear children).[18] God's original command to Adam and Eve, "Be fruitful and multiply, and fill the earth and subdue it,"[19] will come to pass in the way God originally intended it to. No more unwanted babies or starving Asian children; no more abortions, miscarriages, stillbirths, or deformities. Retarded and crippled children will be a thing of the past, and every child born into this world will be a model of health and beauty.

The people born during the Millennium will apparently mature slowly, marrying at the age of 100 or more,[20] and they will live long and peaceful lives of spiritual joy, physical health, and financial prosperity. The phenomenal fertility of the soil will provide more than enough food for all the peoples of the world,[21] and the lack of taxes levied for unemployment, military, and crime-fighting purposes will allow every millennial family on earth to enjoy the highest standard of living in the history of the world.[22] Foster homes and adoption agencies will be interesting relics of the past, and all the hospitals, sanitariums, and rest homes will be closed down forever. Maimed survivors of the Tribulation will be miraculously healed by the King Himself,[23] and every doctor, dentist, and optometrist in the world will have to be retrained for some other profession!

A Zoo Just for You

After Adam and Eve sinned, a hostility emerged between men and animals which exists to this very day. "The fear of you and the terror of you," God told Noah after the flood, "shall be on every beast of the earth and every bird of the sky."[24] And the animals have fought back. Every year thousands of people in various parts of the world die from the bites of snakes, rodents, and insects, and thousands more would die from the attacks of larger animals if it were not for the powerfully destructive impact of man's modern weaponry on the animals of the world. At one time animals were killed or caged in order to protect the people, but now animals are kept in zoos in order to protect the animals!

During the Millennium the entire relationship between man and animals will be revolutionized. People will ride the backs of lions, tigers, and cheetahs, and wolves will compete with collies for the caresses of happy children.[25] Carnivorous animals will be a thing of the past, for bears and cows, lions and oxen will munch grass together in the same verdant pasture.[26]

Will people still kill animals in order to eat their meat? We believe not. In Genesis 1:29 God told Adam and Eve, "Behold, I have given you every plant yielding seed that is on the surface of all the earth, and every tree which has fruit yielding seed; it shall be food for you." A somewhat similar meatless diet was also specified for the animals.[27] The Millennium will apparently be a vegetarian's paradise, with such a rich selection of fruits and vegetables being produced in so many parts of the world that the need for meat in the human diet will be completely eliminated. (Dairy products, however, might continue to be used as protein sources.)

Will the resurrected believers from heaven share meals with the earthly people? We believe they will, just as the resurrected Christ shared meals with His earthly disciples.[28] Remember, our new bodies will be able to function perfectly either in heaven above or on earth below! Unquestionably we will share many hours of happy fellowship with the people on earth in every area of their lives except marriage and procreation.[29]

Rose in the Desert

"Even the wilderness and desert will rejoice in those days," wrote Isaiah; "the desert will blossom with flowers. Yes, there will be an abundance of flowers and singing and joy! The deserts will become as green as the Lebanon Mountains, as lovely as Mount Carmel's pastures and Sharon's meadows, for the Lord will display his glory there, the excellency of our God."[30] Since the early 1950's we have been hearing how Palestine's dry regions have been "blossoming like a rose," but this agricultural renaissance is only a small hint of the fertility of our planet earth in the coming days of the Millennium.

Beginning at Jerusalem and radiating outward to the North and South poles, the blessings of bountiful harvests will overtake our famine-wracked world of today. From the Temple itself will gush out a river that feeds luscious fruit trees all the way from Jerusalem to the Dead Sea.[31] The salty waters of the Dead Sea will become freshened by the tremendous influx of clear water from this new Temple river,[32] and Palestine will enjoy its greatest fisherman's paradise in the history of the land![33]

Farmers all over the world will enjoy unprecendented productivity, and there will be no such thing as a bad year for crops. Agricultural diseases and pests will be gone forever, and so will the diseases and pests that plague mankind itself. There will be no more poverty-stricken dirt farmers or fruit pickers, either; in those days "you will all live in peace and prosperity, and each of you will own a home of your own where you can invite your neighbors."[34]

Goodbye, Sahara!

What will the climate be like in the Millennium? Will the weather of the world be one big happy Hawaii, or will we continue to have 80-below-zero blizzards at the North Pole and 135-degree ovens in the Sahara Desert? We believe the truth lies somewhere in between. Isaiah 35:2 TLB tells us, "The deserts will become as green as the Lebanon Mountains, as lovely as Mount Carmel's pastures and Sharon's meadows," yet Genesis 8:22 says, "While the earth remains, seedtime and harvest, and cold and heat, and summer and winter, and day and night shall not cease."

We believe the Millennium will boast an ideal climate for the various peoples of the world. The northern latitudes will offer striking autumn foliage and a wonderland of winter beauty. There will be skiing and sledding in the winter, but no deaths from numbing winter blizzards, and no lost limbs from frostbite or exposure. In the equatorial latitudes there will no longer be blazing deserts or steaming jungles, but instead pleasant summer weather all year round. We'll be able to swim the sparkling waters of a hundred magnificent shorelines or cruise the storm-free and pollution-free waters of any ocean of the world. Though there will no longer be blazing deserts or deathly northern winters, the various latitudes of the world will still offer enough variety of climate to satisfy even the most sophisticated nature-lover.

The Cancer Cure

"Then the eyes of the blind will be opened, and the ears of the deaf will be unstopped. Then the lame will leap like a deer, and the tongue of the dumb will shout for joy."[35] Though these words of Isaiah were partially fulfilled by the healing ministry of our Lord Jesus Christ on this earth,[36] they will for the first time be *totally* fulfilled in the coming days of the Millennium. Even though the *children* born during the Millennium will be perfect specimens of physical health, many of their *parents* will enter the Millennium with the groans and scars of the premillennial world. It is these adults, some old and sick, and some scarred by the Tribulation horrors, who will need the miraculous healing power of the divine King of the earth.[37]

Not just blindness and deafness, but *every* physical malady of mankind will be corrected by Christ at the very beginning of the Millennium. The medical practitioners among the Tribulation survivors will have to be reeducated for other professions, since millennial life will apparently be free from all physical ailments! Cancer will at last have been conquered, and so will heart disease and diabetes and a hundred other diseases. Children will no longer visit the dentist to get their teeth repaired, and adults will no longer visit him to get their teeth replaced! Headaches, backaches, and low blood sugar will be a thing of the past, and even childbearing will become quick and painless. God's long-term plan for a happy and healthy human population will at last be fully realized!

Even the plants and animals will be healthy.[38] No more veterinarian visits for your puppy or sprayings for your rosebush! All the pests, parasites, germs, and viruses that now plague people, animals, and plants will apparently be gone forever, and physical well-being will become the universal condition of all living things. We don't know whether God will recreate species of animals that have become extinct over the past centuries, but we do know that no additional animals will die out except perhaps for harmful pests and microbes. (Or it is possible that these pests and microbes will be transformed into harmless or even beneficial creatures of God, even as large carnivorous animals will become herbivorous.) In any case, the children of the Millennium will never know what it is to swat a stinging mosquito or to smash a buzzing fly. Their eyes will open in wonder at tales of biting dogs, stinging bees, and deadly cobras. The human agonies of the premillennial age will seem like a bad dream fading into the past.

Ban the Bomb

In the Millennium those famous words will come true, "Then they will hammer their swords into plowshares and their spears into pruning hooks; nation will not lift up sword against nation, and never again will they train for war."[39] In those days our twentieth-century arms race will seem like a nightmare straight out of hell, for the millennial people will not even bother to learn the tactics of warfare, much less build the weapons of destruction.

The military academies at West Point and Annapolis will close down forever, and so will the military schools in every nation of the world.[40] The sophisticated weaponry of the twentieth century will be converted into ultramodern machinery that glorifies God and is useful to mankind. H-bombs will be disarmed and turned into safe, pollution-free nuclear power plants. Supersonic jet fighters will become basic transportation planes for businessmen of the millennial community. Disarmed nuclear submarines will be used to explore the creative wonders of God's good oceans, and ballistic missile launchers will be melted down into sophisticated farm machinery. The technology of the Millennium will be superb, far advanced from our own today, but all of it will bring glory to God and blessing to the people.

The pollution problems that plague our world today will be solved in a few months of ultramodern cleanup technology. Nuclear wastes will be deactivated by effective techniques not yet known by present-day research physicists. Automobiles will finally be made completely pollution-free, and the beautiful factories of the world will glisten in the sparkling-pure air of the rebuilt cities. Young people will launch worldwide campaigns to pick up the billions of beer cans and cigarette wrappers left behind by the calloused polluters of the premillennial era, and God's good earth will once again be fresh and clean.

America the Beautiful

Even though Jerusalem and Palestine will be the center of worship and government in the Millennium,[41] *every* nation in the world will be ruled by Christ and will enjoy His blessing.[42] For the first time in her history the United States will become all those things which she has dreamed of becoming from the day of her founding. Now at last there will be true liberty and justice for all, and poverty and unemployment will be conquered forever. All the people of the nation will be healthy and well-fed, and no child will ever again be born unloved or unwanted. Corruption in high places will be a thing of the past, and conflicts between employer and employee will be found only in history texts. Crime will be virtually nonexistent, and the inner-city slums will be converted into beautiful residential homes and parks.

The lakes and rivers of the nation will once again become sparkling retreats for bathers and fishermen, and the national parks will be frequented by courteous visitors who respect the creation of God and the rights of other people. For the first time the vacation scenery will match the descriptions of the travel agencies' brochures, and people will marvel at the country's rapid recovery from the horrors of the Tribulation. In those days America will realize the full meaning of the words,

> O beautiful for spacious skies,
>   for amber waves of grain,
> For purple-mountained majesties
>   above the fruited plain!

America, America!
God shed His grace on thee,
And crown thy good with brotherhood
from sea to shining sea![43]

How About You?

These glowing descriptions of the millennial
world are not just hyped-up fantasies. They are factual details of the real world that the Creator of the
universe will implement after the seven terrible
years of the coming Tribulation period. People who
receive Christ now and are taken up to heaven at the
time of the Rapture will never experience the
Tribulation horrors at all,[44] but will enter directly
into the blessings of the millennial world as soon as
the Tribulation on earth is over.[45] People who
become saved after the Rapture and during the
Tribulation will either die as martyrs for their faith
or will survive the Tribulation despite terrible
persecution.[46] If they die before the end of the
Tribulation, they will first go to heaven,[47] and then
(after Christ's return to earth at the end of the
Tribulation) they will enter the Millennium as
resurrected saints,[48] living in the heavenly city and
commuting to their daily rulership responsibilities
on earth. Those post-Rapture believers who *survive*
the Tribulation will enter the Millennium as
nonresurrected followers of Christ and will live
idealized human lives in the millennial world.[49] For
an easy-to-understand chart of these events, see
Guide to the New World on page 140.

Those people who have rejected the good news

about Christ and His salvation before the Rapture will continue to harden their hearts once the Rapture has taken place.[50] If you have read this book up to this point, you can no longer claim ignorance of God's way of salvation through the Lord Jesus Christ. You must either receive Him as your Savior before the Rapture or else risk overwhelming deception by the Antichrist once the Rapture has taken place. Every day before the Rapture hundreds of people around the world are rethinking their rejection of Christ and are receiving Him as their Savior. Today you still have that opportunity. Use it while you can.

Chapter 9

SUPER-RIOT

When the thousand years are completed, Satan will be released from his prison, and will come out to deceive the nations which are in the four corners of the earth . . . to gather them together for the war. The number of them is like the sand of the seashore.

—Revelation 20:7, 8

The history of Satan is a fascinating one. Long before Adam and Eve ever saw the light of day, Lucifer walked with God as the radiant son of the morning. "Full of wisdom and perfect in beauty," he led millions of angels in worshipful service to their Creator-God.[1]

But then something happened. Somehow Lucifer envisioned himself as more than just the highest of God's created beings. With welling pride he said to himself, "I will ascend to heaven; I will raise my throne above the stars of God, and I will sit on the mount of assembly in the recesses of the north. I will ascend above the heights of the clouds; I will make myself like the Most High."[2] God's creatorial gifts of wisdom, power, and beauty became a source of pride to Lucifer, and he presumed to think that he could rise above God Himself. But Satan was not alone in his presumptuous rebellion; millions of other angels apparently followed Lucifer's leadership in rebelling against the God of heaven.[3]

Fallen Angels

"How you have fallen from heaven," laments Isaiah, "O star of the morning, son of the dawn! You have been cut down to the earth, you who have weakened the nations!"[4] The holy God of heaven will brook no rival in His perfect rulership of the universe. This is not pride, but justice, since the overthrow of a perfect Ruler by a less-than-perfect one would be the ultimate calamity of eternity. And in any case the overthrow of the infinitely powerful God of creation by any finite created being, no matter how impressive his gifts of power or beauty, would be an utter impossibility.[5] Despite all his God-given brilliance, Lucifer had embarked on the most irrational fiasco of all time or eternity.

As far as we can tell from Scripture, this act of rebellion was the first sin committed in the entire history of the universe. Because of the seriousness of this crime, no hope for the redemption of fallen angels is offered anywhere in the Bible. Instead, at the end of the Millennium they will be consigned to the lake of fire and "tormented day and night forever and ever."[6] Rebellion against the holy and loving God of heaven is the most serious sin which any created being can commit.

During the many centuries between Satan's expulsion from heaven and his ultimate consignment to the lake of fire, he and his fallen angels have been allowed a limited amount of liberty in and around our world. They have lost their beautiful angelic bodies as part of the punishment for their sin, and now they hunt desperately for earthly bodies in which to live. They prefer idol images (so that people will bow down and worship them, whether knowingly or unknowingly),[7] and they also enjoy living in the bodies of human recipients when possible.[8] If necessary, they will settle for the bodies of certain kinds of animals,[9] or they will even live in trees or houses. (Haunted houses are inhabited by demons whose human hosts have died, leaving the demons only an empty house in which to live. These demons resent new human inhabitants for the "haunted house" unless these people are also willing to become demon-possessed.)

When Adam and Eve sinned, Satan gained partial control over the world that Adam once ruled fully. The remainder of the control is shared by the human race and supervised by God Himself. There is therefore a continuing three-way struggle between God, man, and Satan for the control of the world and its people. God will of course be the ultimate Winner of this agelong conflict,[10] but in the meantime Satan exerts heavy influence over the affairs of men:"Our struggle is not against flesh and blood, but against the rulers, against the powers, against the world-forces of this darkness, against the spiritual forces of wickedness in the heavenly places."[11]

The Devil Made Me Do It?

Satan works in the world today by means of

three primary tactics—direct assault, deception, and religious imitation.[12] All three methods have proven extremely effective in getting people to reject the truth about God and His sacrificial provision for our salvation. People all over the world choose demonically slanted propaganda and literature ("doctrines of demons")[13] instead of turning to the Lord Jesus Christ in personal repentance and faith. Millions of educated and uneducated people deliberately reject the truth about God and pay the consequences with eternal spiritual death.[14]

Yet in the coming day of judgment no man can truthfully say to God, "The devil made me do it." Through the power of God's Holy Spirit each of us has the ability to choose Christ instead of Satan.[15]

Foretaste of Hell

Despite all his brilliant temptational tactics, Satan has difficulty in getting large numbers of people to actually worship him. He is reasonably successful in robbing God of the earthly human worship that belongs to Him, but Satan is much less successful in actually obtaining worship for himself. The number of outright Satan worshipers in Western society today is not staggeringly large in spite of the recent surge of interest in demonic and occultic matters.

But in the coming Tribulation the picture will be different. Before the Tribulation is over, all the people in the world will be required to bow in worship to the Satan-filled Antichrist or else pay for their refusal with the risk of their lives.[16] Most people will reluctantly comply; only Christ's loyal post-Rapture converts will stand up to the edict of the Beast, and many of these will be murdered for their loyalty to Christ.[17] For the first and last time in the history of the world, Satan will be receiving that massive homage from mankind which he has been grasping after all these many centuries.

And for the first time in human history the people of the world will see what the kingship of Satan is really like. The brutality of Hitler's armies will pale in comparison to the blood-lust of the Satan-filled Beast. The groaning world will cry out for some kind of human deliverance from this tyrannical Beast, but all those people who rejected the true King of the world will instead get their foretaste of hell from the phony sovereign himself. If it were not for the timely return of Christ shortly before the full seven years of the Tribulation have elapsed, the entire human population of the earth would be decimated: "For then there will be a great tribulation, such as has not occurred since the beginning of the world until now, nor ever shall. And unless those days had been cut short, no life would have been saved; but for the sake of the elect those days shall be cut short."[18]

Into the Pit

When Christ returns to earth with His armies from heaven at the end of the Tribulation, He will not only slaughter the millions of human rebels on earth, but He will also throw Satan's Antichrist and False Prophet alive into the lake of fire, and our present era of human rebellion against God will have come to an end.[19] Satan himelf will be consigned to the abyss by a powerful angel from heaven, and there he will remain for the entire thousand-year duration of the Millennium.[20] Now at last the human race will be free to worship and serve God untempted by the master deceiver.

Right now we are tempted by "the world, the flesh, and the devil," that is, the sinful world around us, our own sinful natures inside us, and Satan and his demons.[21] Of course Satan *personally* does not bother to tempt most of us, since his actual presence is limited to one place at a time, and this limited personal presence must be concentrated on the most influential Christian leaders of the moment.[22] But millions of demons of various ranks do personally tempt all of us who are doing anything worthwhile for Christ.[23] During the Millennium neither Satan nor his demons will be able to harrass the people of earth,[24] and the general human environment will be one of peace, love, and joy.[25] This would result in a totally perfect condition of paradise except for one important fact: the sin-nature of man himself.[26]

The Worm in the Apple

"All have sinned and come short of the glory of God," Paul tells us in Romans 3:23, and John the Apostle adds, "If we say we have no sin we deceive ourselves, and the truth is not in us. . . . If we say we have not sinned we make Him a liar, and His Word is not in us."[27] Ever since Adam and Eve disobeyed God in the Garden of Eden, the human race has been infected with this terrible disease called sin. Young and old, rich and poor, *everyone* is guilty of violating the holiness of God.[28]

When we get to heaven through either death or the Rapture we will sin no more, for "we shall be like Him, for we shall see Him as He is."[29] But the *nonresurrected survivors of the Tribulation* will not yet have their glorified bodies or sinless natures. Even as Christ's true believers today fail conspicuously in their Christian lives at times, so the earthly believers in Christ's millennial kingdom will also have their weaknesses and failures.[30]

But even more important than this fact is the phenomenon of the millennial children. The babies of the Millennium will be born with Adamic sin-natures, just as babies are born today, and all the children of the Millennium will need to receive Christ as their personal Savior if they ever expect to spend eternity with Him.[31] Most of the millennial children will make this wise and right decision, but some of them will make the wrong choice in spite of their beautiful and near-ideal environment.[32] Just as Lucifer, son of the morning, had no excuse whatever for rising up in rebellion against his loving Creator, so these millennial rebels will someday stand without excuse before the Great White Throne of God in heaven.[33]

As the years pass in the Millennium, these physically healthy unbelievers will grow up, marry unbelievers, and establish unbelieving families of their own. After a century or two, every nation in the world will have a significant minority of these unsaved citizens.[34]

The Good Old Days?

These unsaved people will start to mutter and complain against the holy rule of Christ and His subordinate officers throughout the world: "Let us tear their fetters apart and cast away their cords from us!"[35] Rumors will make the rounds about "the good old days" in the U.S.A., when people were allowed to do anything they wanted to as long as they "weren't hurting anybody." And freedom of the press—where is that freedom of the press which the Americans used to have? Sure, there are thousands of millennial books, magazines, and newspapers that explore sacred and secular information from God's point of view, but where is the freedom to blaspheme God and get away with it?[36] And how about radio and TV freedom? How about an atheistic program once in a while? And how about that zealous law enforcement? Steal a few dollars from your neighbor's unlocked house, and the very next day two government rulers demand immediate restitution for the victim of the crime![37] As the centuries of the Millennium roll on, this growing minority of millennial rebels will multiply into a powerful tide of malevolent discontent.[38]

The Rod of Iron

God's response to the mutterings of the malcontents will be swift and stern: "He who sits in the heavens laughs; the Lord scoffs at them. Then He will speak to them in His anger and terrify them in His fury: 'But as for Me, I have installed My King upon Zion, My holy mountain. . . . Ask of Me, and I will surely give the nations as Thine inheritance, and the very ends of the earth as Thy possession. Thou shalt break them with a rod of iron, Thou shalt shatter them like earthenware. Now therefore, O kings, show discernment; take warning, O judges of the earth. Worship the Lord with reverence, and rejoice with trembling. Do homage to the Son, lest He become angry and you perish in the way.' "[39]

God will put up with no nonsense during the millennial rule of Christ. Holiness will be the hallmark of the earth from China to Jerusalem. Let the rebels mutter as they will, Christ will continue to rule with love and justice from His capitol in Jerusalem.[40] Crime will be punished swiftly and surely,[41] and no community in the world will fear for their lives at any time of night or day. Minor offenders will be required to make immediate restitution for their crimes, while major offenders will pay for their sins with immediate and just punishment, including capital punishment for certain offenses.[42]

The billions of believers throughout the millennial world will rejoice at the holiness of God maintained by swift and sure retribution,[43] but the rebel hordes will only deepen their hatred against the holy King of the world. Even as the religious sinners of Palestine hated Christ for His holiness two thousand years ago, so the future sinners of the Millennium will hate Him for doing what is right and fair.[44] The showdown is unavoidable, and Christ is willing to take on all comers.

The Great Revolt

In the final conflict of good and evil in the whole long history of the world, God will release Satan from the abyss to do what he will with the rebels of the world. Here is what he will do: "Satan will be released from his prison, and will come out to deceive the nations which are in the four corners of the earth, Gog and Magog, to gather them together for the war; the number of them is like the sand of the seashore. And they came up on the broad plain of the earth and surrounded the camp of the saints and the beloved city."[45]

Even in Christ's millennial paradise there will be millions of people ready to rise up in rebellion at the holy King of the world! But this time no "gentle Jesus" will submit to the humiliations of His rebellious creatures. Instead, He will give them exactly what they deserve—the consuming fire from heaven.[46] Both Satan and the millennial rebels will be "thrown into the lake of fire and brimstone . . . and they will be tormented day and night forever and ever."[47] Now the world will be rid forever of rebellion to the perfect rule of the Creator. Now the age-long conflict between good and evil will end in eternal triumph for the triune God of heaven.

Chapter 10

GUILTY!

If anyone's name was not found written in the book of life, he was thrown into the lake of fire.

—Revelation 20:15

The Great White Throne judgment is one of the most awesome events in all of cosmic history. "It is appointed unto men once to die," warns God in Hebrews 9:27, "but after this the judgment."[1] From firstborn Cain to the endtime rebels of the millennial world, corrupt human beings have faced judgment for their sins and eternal separation from God.

How is it that a loving Father in heaven can consign fallible human beings to an eternity of suffering and punishment? Though this question has been asked by millions of people down through the history of the world, it is actually the wrong question to ask. The right question is, "How is it that a just and holy God has been willing to put up with the sins of His rebellious creatures for all these many centuries?" The same Bible which tells us "God is love"[2] also tells us "God is light, and in Him is no darkness at all."[3] When we really understand who God is, we cry out with the living creatures in heaven, "Holy, holy, holy is the Lord God, the Almighty, who was, and who is, and who is to come!"[4]

The True God

Many of us have been brainwashed by twentieth-century propaganda into believing that God in heaven is some kind of patronizing old grandpa who smiles at the shortcomings of the people on earth and dismisses their sins with a wink and a nod. If we try real hard, we think, we'll do more good things than bad things, and the nice Old Man in the sky will tell St. Peter to open the pearly gates for us.

What an insult to the suffering and death of the Son of God Himself! If we could make it to heaven by our own good works, why did Christ have to bear the sins of the world at the Cross of Calvary? [5] No human being who rejects the sacrificial love of Christ will ever see the face of God in heaven, no matter how pious a facade he may be erecting in his life: "He who does not obey the Son shall not see life, but the wrath of God abides on him."[6] Since both the love of God and the holiness of God are infinite, any person who rejects the love of God by spurning the sacrifice of Christ will taste only the blazing holiness of God for the rest of eternity.[7]

God is no fool; if people do not want to glorify Him by drinking in His love, they will nevertheless glorify Him by drinking in His punishment, since God receives glory for His holiness when He punishes sinners justly in hell.[8] But God receives *far greater glory* when He showers *both holiness and love* upon all the redeemed saints in heaven, and that is why God longs for you to revel in His gracious love forever.[9] Why settle for His holiness poured out in hell when you can enjoy His love in heaven forever?

The Great Surprise

Sometime shortly after the great uprising at the end of the Millennium, there will be a colossal event that surprises millions of unsaved people waiting in hades for the great day of judgment. (Hades is the presentencing abode of the lost, and some of its details are described in Luke 16:19-31, the true account of the rich man in hades.) That great surprise will be the resurrection of the damned: "Many who sleep in the dust of the earth will awake," wrote Daniel, "some to everlasting life and others to shame and everlasting contempt."[10] John the Apostle adds, "I saw the dead, the great and the small, standing before the throne . . . . And the sea gave up the dead which were in it, and death and hades gave up the dead which were in them. And they were judged, every one of them, according to their deeds."[11]

But why a resurrection of the damned? Is it not enough that *believers* receive new bodies forever? The answer is twofold. While believers will receive new bodies which "shine like the stars forever and ever,"[12] *unbelievers* will receive new bodies which are physically and mentally whole but are not particularly beautiful. It is in these whole bodies with perfectly functioning minds that unbelievers will endure their just punishment and separation from God forever. No unbeliever in the prison of hell will ever be able to stab himself to death or gas himself to oblivion, for his resurrected body will be *physically* immortal in spite of his eternal spiritual separation from God. This is the ultimate tragedy of hell.

But there is another reason for the resurrection of both saved and unsaved people, and that is to display forever the creatorial power and wisdom of God. The human body is a masterpiece of divine science and engineering,[13] and even the lost people in hell will never shake a crippled arm against the holy Creator in heaven!

The Great White Throne

Before God's Great White Throne will stand millions of people from all eras of world history.[14] Unless he secretly repented in his last moments of life on earth, Adolf Hitler will be there, and so will Adolf Eichmann and Joseph Stalin and dozens of other mass murderers of World War Two.[15] All those clever atheists who had their bodies cremated after death in order to escape the resurrecting power of God will stand silently in the presence of the Almighty. All those deceptive leaders of Communism, atheism, and relativism will wait silently while the Source of all truth hands down His sentence of justice.[16]

But other people will be there too—ordinary people who have never murdered anyone or deceived the masses, but who have rejected the truth of God's love as shown in Jesus Christ.[17] These will be the people who either rejected God's love outright or else decided to work their way to heaven on the basis of their own good deeds. These are the people who disbelieved God when He said, "All have sinned and come short of the glory of God"[18] and "Not by works of righteousness which we have done, but according to His mercy He saved us, by the washing of regeneration and renewing of the Holy Spirit, which He shed on us abundantly through Jesus Christ our Savior."[19] Too late these people will realize that God means exactly what He says in His written Scriptures.

How About the Heathen?

But how about the people who have never seen the Bible and have never heard the good news about salvation through the death of Christ? Will these innocent people be condemned to hell too? In the first place, no human being is innocent in the sight of God.[20] In the legal sense, all of us are guilty of participating in the original sin of Adam,[21] and in the practical sense all of us have committed hundreds or thousands of outright acts of sin against God.[22] Before we are born again into God's family, the thought-life of all of us is one boiling cauldron of jealousy, slander, lust, and even murder.[23] We may be reasonably successful in hiding our inner thoughts from the people around us, but the omniscient God of the universe knows exactly what is going on inside our minds.[24]

The jungle tribesmen of Africa or South America may look like peaceful berrypickers to the casual visitor, but both God and the natives themselves know that they have a serious problem of

113

sin.[25] One of the phenomena that led to the conversion of C. S. Lewis, the late British author, was his observation that every heathen tribe he ever studied fell short of meeting even its own low standards of conscience. The heathen know they are sinners, but almost all of them reject the remedy that is available to them.[26]

What is this remedy? God has revealed His power and deity to all peoples of the world through the glory of His creation.[27] In addition, all people in the world are born with a God-given conscience which enables them to tell the basic difference between right and wrong.[28] It is true that the consciences of natives can be bent and twisted by local traditions,[29] but it is also true that God the Holy Spirit is at work around the world, retarding the full development of worldwide sin and influencing people to repent of their own personal sins.[30]

Like Abraham the patriarch, Naaman the leper, and Nebuchadnezzar the king, if a person responds to all the knowledge that is available to him, "this will be counted to him for righteousness."[31] Missionaries from around the world report that on rare occasions they meet unevangelized natives who have repented of their sins and received the revelation of God that is available to them through creation and conscience (with perhaps a supplementary vision also).

But such people are extremely rare; most heathen natives reject the light of God's creation, the quiet working of the Holy Spirit, and the inner workings of their own conscience, and instead they turn to the worship of manmade idols.[32] For this deliberate rejection of the triple witness available to them, the overwhelming majority of heathen live and die as lost unbelievers.[33]

If a born-again missionary brings the good news of Christ to these heathen people, a much larger minority of them will respond to this dramatic story of God's grace and will become new creatures in Christ Jesus. That is why thousands of Christians obey the call of the Holy Spirit to go out to the mission fields of the world with the dramatic good news about Christ.[34] Tens of thousands of heathen unbelievers who *reject* the threefold witness of creation, conscience, and the Holy Spirit will *receive* the overwhelming impact of God the Son dying on the Cross for their sins.[35] We therefore do not go to the mission field to rescue people who are unjustly being sent to hell; we go there to change the minds of rebellious sinners who deserve to be eternally separated from God. Since all of us were once rebellious sinners ourselves, we go to the unchurched with an attitude of gracious humility rather than one of personal pride.[36]

But You Have Heard

Regardless of your views about the unevangelized people of the world, you can no longer consider yourself one of them. If you have read this book up to this point, you are responsible to make an intelligent decision in favor of Christ. You can no longer claim only a threefold witness to the revelation of God (creation, conscience, and the quiet inner working of the Holy Spirit). You have now seen the one stupendous revelation of God to which all three of these related witnesses point: the sacrificial death and resurrection of God the Son Himself.[37] If you reject such love, God has no choice but to consign you to hell forever.[38]

Even as the jungle native is required to receive *all* the revelation of God that is available to him, so you too must receive *all you now know* about God's love in Christ Jesus if you ever hope to make it to heaven.[39] "Believing in God" is not the same as receiving Jesus Christ as your personal Savior. James tells us that even the demons "believe and tremble,"[40] yet they will spend all eternity in hell. *You must receive Christ as your personal Savior*, and you must do it soon.

The Books and the Book

When the unsaved people from every era of world history stand before God's Great White Throne in heaven, certain books will be opened in their presence: "I saw the dead, the great and the small, standing before the throne, and books were opened . . . ."[41] What is written in these books? The earthly deeds of condemned sinners: "The dead were judged from the things which were written in the books, according to their deeds."[42]

This is the hour when every criminal in the world will finally receive the full punishment he deserves. Every murderer, every rapist, every kidnapper who has died unsaved will stand silently as God spells out the crimes he has committed and the sentence which will be passed.[43] No Clarence Darrow will rise up to trick the Judge with clever courtroom ploys. No overlooked technicality will compel the court to set the guilty free, for every legal procedure will have been perfectly executed by the Master Prosecutor Himself. Nor will there be any false charges or frame-ups. No one will pay for the sins of any other human being.[44]

But not just murderers and rapists will stand in that holy hall of justice; millions of ordinary people will be there too. It is not necessary to murder your neighbor in order to be banished from the presence of God; rejecting the love of Christ is more than adequate reason.[45]

"Another book was opened, which is the book of life . . . ."[46] What is this Book of Life? It is the final evidence of the courtroom scene, showing that no defendant is listed in this roll of the redeemed, and that no defendant has any valid claim to eternal life. The name of every born-again believer is written forever in God's "Book of Life,"[47] but the name of every unsaved person will be tragically absent from this register of the redeemed.[48] As this Book is reviewed on that great day of reckoning, every convicted sinner will see for himself that his name is indeed missing from that fateful Book of Life. What a trauma of horror on that day of the damned!

The Lake of Fire

After the sentencing is over, the horror of hell itself will await every prisoner who has appeared at God's Great White Throne. Until now every prisoner will have been held in a preliminary place of punishment called hades (see Luke 16:19-31), but now each convict will face the agony of the lake of fire itself: "If anyone's name was not found written in the book of life, he was thrown into the lake of fire."[49]

Many true things and many false things have been said about the lake of fire. In the first place, every Christ-rejector will be there for all eternity. If God was willing to submit His own Son to the hell of Calvary's Cross for your sins, you can be sure He will be willing to confine you to hell's punishment forever if you reject such an overwhelming display of Calvary love.[50] This awesome fact ought to make all of us search our hearts to see if we have truly received Christ as our Savior.

Yet to be truly fair, God will tailor the *intensity* of His punishments to fit the guilt of each individual in hell. That is the meaning of the words "the dead were judged from the things which were written in the books, according to their deeds."[51] That is also the meaning of such words as "that servant who knew his Lord's will and prepared not himself, neither did according to his will, shall be beaten with many stripes. But he who knew not and did commit things worthy of stripes shall be beaten with few stripes."[52] The unevangelized sinners of Sodom and Gomorrah will suffer a less severe punishment in hell than the people who have heard about the love of Christ but have rejected Him anyway.[53] This same lesser punishment will also be imposed on the comparatively ignorant sinners of Tyre and Sidon,[54] since God judges the severity of a person's guilt partly on the extent of his spiritual knowledge.[55]

Yet hell will not be pleasant for anyone. Though the rich man in hades had been greedy and selfish during his earthly life, he had apparently never murdered or raped anyone, yet his suffering in hades was quite severe.[56] Other passages of Scripture talk about "weeping, wailing, and gnashing of teeth."[57]

On the other hand, the suffering in hell will not be intolerable in the technical sense of the word, since everyone who is there will endure his just punishment forever. Though the *duration* of the suffering in hell will be infinite, the *intensity* of the suffering will be finite (though great), since an infinite intensity of suffering would annihilate any finite sufferer.

It is not God's purpose to *annihilate* sinners (which they might prefer), but to punish them with perfect fairness for all the sins they have committed against Him. No one in hell will be punished one bit too severely, and no one will be punished one bit too leniently. Each person will receive exactly the right degree of suffering that he deserves for his sins.

Is there real fire in hell? We believe there is. The rich man in hades said, "I am tormented in this flame,"[58] and the very term "lake of fire"[59] carries an awesome impact. But even if the fire were figurative, this should bring us little comfort, since the realities of Scripture are never less forceful than the figures of speech which portray these realities. Hell is truly a terrible place, and not one of us should be willing to go there. God Himself longs to see as many people as possible repent of their sins and turn in faith to Jesus Christ, the Savior of sinners.[60] Nothing would please God more than to see you make this decision today.

Chapter 11

HAPPY NEW WORLD

I saw a new heaven and a new earth, for the first earth had passed away.... And there shall no longer be any death; there shall no longer be any mourning or crying or pain, for the first things have passed away.

—*Revelation 21:1, 4*

"In the beginning God created the heavens and the earth." With these majestic words the Bible begins, and with these words we open a hornet's nest of controversy. How long ago was this "beginning" of Genesis 1:1, and what process did God use to create the universe? Is the rest of Genesis chapter 1 a description of this original creation, or does it describe a much more recent renovation of earth and sky? Without explaining our lengthy technical reasons at the moment, we believe that the original creation of the universe took place many thousands or millions of years ago, but that the ancient planet earth was plunged into darkness and ruin at the time of Lucifer's rebellion against God many thousands of years ago.[1]

Sometime after this event (probably only six to eight thousand years ago) God renovated the earth in the six literal days of creative activity described in

Genesis 1:2-31. The Genesis narrative skips over the time gap between the first two verses of the book because the sequence of events which took place during this period does not relate directly to our present world at all. (Many historical facts which are intriguing but not especially relevant to our spiritual well-being have been deliberately left unstated by the Holy Spirit, the ultimate Author of the Bible.)

In other words, the basic *constituent materials* of our earth are probably many thousands or millions of years old, but the *present vital processes* of our earth were initiated only a few thousand years ago.

Rebirth of the Earth

But there will also be a future cataclysmic renovation of the millennial earth and sky, and this time every human being in the universe will witness the event: "The present heavens and earth by His word are being reserved for fire, kept for the day of judgment and destruction of ungodly men . . . . The day of the Lord will come like a thief, in which the heavens will pass away with a roar and the elements will be destroyed with intense heat, and the earth and its works will be burned up. Since all these things are to be destroyed in this way, what sort of people ought you to be in holy conduct and godliness, looking for and hastening the coming of the day of God, on account of which the heavens will be destroyed by burning and the elements will melt with intense heat! But according to His promise we are looking for new heavens and a new earth, in which righteousness dwells. Therefore, beloved, since you look for these things, be diligent to be found by Him in peace, spotless and blameless."[2]

After His Great White Throne Judgment, God will destroy the planet earth and our entire solar system in a tremendous holocaust of fire. Even though the millennial world will have been idyllic in many ways, the rebellious acts and attitudes of a large minority of its citizens, culminating in the final Satan-led revolution, will have rendered the earth and sky unsuitable as a truly flawless environment for the holy God, His holy angels, and His holy people. But once all the rebels of the universe have been consigned to hell forever, God will create a new heavens and a new earth "in which dwelleth righteousness."[3]

No Time for Tears

The new world will be a tearless society, for all the sorrows of the past will be forgotten, and the present and the future will offer nothing but love, joy, and peace: "Behold, the tabernacle of God is among men, and He shall dwell among them, and they shall be His peoples, and God Himself shall be among them, and He shall wipe away every tear from their eyes, and there shall no longer be any death. There shall no longer be any mourning or crying or pain: the first things have passed away."[4]

While the *millennial* society will have been happy in *most* respects, the *eternal* society will be totally blissful in *all* respects. No rebel will ever again rise up to challenge the power of God, and no redeemed saint will ever again witness an act of sin or rebellion anywhere in the universe. The triune Godhead—not just the Lord Jesus Christ, but God the Father and God the Holy Spirit as well—will personally live with the redeemed people of the new world.[5] Christ and His people will continue their millennial rulership, except that God the Father Himself will once again become the official King of the universe.[6] (Christ's previous thousand-year kingship during the Millennium will have been awarded to Him partially as a compensation for the unspeakable humiliation which He suffered at the hands of His own rebellious creatures.)[7]

In the eternal new world we will in some way see the face of God the Father as well as that of the Lord Jesus Christ, for "the throne of God and of the Lamb shall be in it, and His bondservants shall serve Him, and they shall see His face, and His name shall be on their foreheads."[8] As great as our face-to-face fellowship with the Son of God will have been during the glorious years of the Millennium, it will be even greater with the triune God during the endless ages of eternity. This is the ultimate joy of the universe for all of us who have come to God by faith in Jesus Christ.

The New Jerusalem

"I saw the holy city, new Jerusalem, coming down out of heaven from God, made ready as a bride adorned for her husband."[9] We believe that this city has existed in heaven from at least the time of Christ's resurrection, and probably as early as the days of Abraham or even earlier. It is to this beautiful heavenly city that all of Christ's believers go at the time of death or the Rapture. This is the "Father's house" of John 14:2 and the "city of the living God, the heavenly Jerusalem" of Hebrews 12:22.

From the day of its construction by God Himself, this city has been a completely tangible and indescribably beautiful place in which to live. Unlike our temporary cities of earth, this heavenly city will be one of the few nonliving things to survive God's end-time renovation of the physical earth and sky. (The other living and nonliving survivors will include holy and sinful angels, saved and unsaved people, the written Word of God, and of course the triune Creator Himself.) The New Jerusalem is described as "a bride adorned for her husband"[10] because the bride of Christ (the church) lives in this city, and also because the earthly believers of the millennial world will be seeing its beauties for the first time here at the beginning of the renovated world. (These long-lived earthly believers will now go to heaven for the first time and will now have their hardy earthly bodies upgraded to fully immortal, resurrection-type bodies similar to those of the believers taken up to heaven at the time of the Rapture.)

Transparent Gold

Fifteen hundred miles square and fifteen hundred miles high,[11] the New Jerusalem will be larger than the entire western half of the United

States. The city will rest on the new earth atop twelve overlaying foundations composed of twelve of the most beautiful and valuable minerals ever known to men or angels.[12] The jasper wall will be over two hundred feet high, and the streets of the city will be made of a special transparent gold.[13]

Instead of a physical temple, the New Jerusalem will have God the Father and God the Son as its center of worship, and they will also provide its eternal illumination: "I saw no temple in it, for the Lord God, the Almighty, and the Lamb are its temple; and the city has no need of the sun or of the moon to shine upon it, for the glory of God has illumined it, and its lamp is the Lamb."[14] Is this description literal? Is this really what God's eternal city will look like? We can think of no reason whatever to reject a straightforward interpretation of these verses of Scripture. If the Bible means what it says, this eternal city will be more tangible and permanent than any present-day city of earth.[15]

Nations Forever

After the New Jerusalem descends to the new earth, a very interesting phenomenon seems to take place: part of the population of the city continues to live within its walls, while another part of the population relocates to the perfect new earth.[16] The twelve gates inscribed with "the twelve tribes of the sons of Israel"[17] suggest that born-again *Jewish* people (those Jews saved before or after the church era) will continue to live in the New Jerusalem, while the twelve foundation stones inscribed with "the twelve names of the twelve apostles of the Lamb"[18] imply that the *church* believers will remain there too. But Revelation 21:24-26 describes the following interesting information about the eternal new world *surrounding* the New Jerusalem: "The nations shall walk by its light, and the kings of the earth shall bring their glory into it. And in the daytime (for there shall be no night there) its gates shall never be closed; and they shall bring the glory and the honor of the nations into it."

Apparently all *Gentiles* who were saved either before or after the church era will live eternally in the new world surrounding the New Jerusalem. People like Enoch, Noah, Naaman the leper, and Nebuchadnezzar the king, for example, will apparently live in this beautiful new world rather than inside the city proper. There will be a harmonious interchange of fellowship between these three major groups of believers, for "the kings of the earth shall bring their glory into it . . . . Its gates shall never be closed, and they shall bring the glory and the honor of the nations into it."[19] And of course the Jewish and church saints who live inside the city will have free access to the entire new world as well as to the rest of the universe.

The Real Star Trek

"The heavens declare the glory of God, and the firmament showeth His handiwork,"[20] wrote David as he looked into the starry skies over Palestine. Hundreds of verses of Scripture are devoted to the glory of God in creation, and we will continue to marvel at the magnificence of God's handiwork even after we get to heaven. In heaven the elders will worship God with the words, "Worthy art Thou, our Lord and our God, to receive glory and honor and power, for Thou didst create all things, and because of Thy will they existed and were created."[21]

Since we will no longer be earthbound by our present mortal bodies, we will undoubtedly be able to visit any part of God's universe that we wish to. At first there will be guided tours by the angels, since they are already thoroughly familiar not only with the raw facts about the universe but also with God's perfect reasons for creating each individual heavenly object. (We know the angels are familiar with the heavenly bodies because occasionally a fallen angel will disclose advanced information about our solar system during a spiritistic seance.) Our present-day planetary explorations will seem like children's games when compared with our future freedom to explore the vast reaches of God's perfect universe.

But how about the people in hell? Will they also be able to enjoy the beauties of God's creation? We believe not. Matthew 25:30 tells us, "Cast out the worthless slave into the outer darkness; in that place there shall be weeping and gnashing of teeth." One of the great tragedies of hell is that education and enlightenment will be withheld from its inhabitants forever. Even now the people in hades probably have no knowledge of the great scientific advances made in our world during the past several centuries, and the sufferers in that future lake of fire will probably never know what the New Jerusalem, the new world, and the new universe are all about. They may realize that "out there" is a place of joy and happiness, even as the rich man in hades saw Abraham with Lazarus in his bosom,[22] but they will remain eternally ignorant of the details of God's new world and the blessings of eternal life.[23] May God help you to opt for eternal life through Jesus Christ our Lord rather than eternal ignorance in the outer darkness of hell.

Chapter 12

FOREVER ALIVE

These things I have written to you who believe in the name of the Son of God, in order that you may know that you have eternal life.

—1 John 5:13

Let's review for a moment. (You may wish to refer to the *Guide to the New World* chart on page 140.) If a born-again Christian dies before the Rapture, he is carried by the angels to heaven and is welcomed there by the people he has directly or indirectly won to Christ.[1] He receives a special body which functions perfectly in heaven but is not yet capable of returning to the world below.[2] His fellowship with Christ and his joy in heaven are great,[3] but he continues to look forward to even greater events to come.[4]

The Rapture and Resurrection

The next great event is the Rapture, when Christ will descend from the heavenly city to the clouds above the earth with a personal shout of victory accompanied by the triumphant voice of the archangel and the piercing trumpet-call of God.[5] The previously deceased saints from heaven will return to the earth to receive their newly resurrected bodies from the millions of freshly opened graves, and the bodies of the Christians still living on the earth will be instantly transformed into beautiful, resurrection-type bodies.[6] After a brief reunion on earth, the living and the once-deceased believers will rise together as a fellowshiping group to meet Christ in the clouds above.[7] Then this immense group of newly glorified believers will accompany Christ to the New Jerusalem, their beautiful and tangible home forever.[8] (During the Millennium the heavenly believers will commute regularly to their earthly rulership duties,[9] and after the renovation of the physical universe [at the end of the Millennium] this heavenly city will descend to the new earth.[10] But at no time from death or the Rapture onward will any heavenly believer give up residence in the heavenly city, except for the saved "nations" in the postmillennial renovation.)[11]

After the Rapture

After the Rapture will begin the seven-year Tribulation period described so graphically in the Bible.[12] Half the human population will die from the wars, famines, and plagues of this period,[13] and the remainder of the *unbelievers* will be killed at the end of the Tribulation by Christ as the returning Warrior from heaven.[14] (The believers in heaven will keep track of the unfolding drama of the Tribulation with an attitude of awe and worship, glorifying God for His holy justice displayed on the earth.)[15]

At the very end of the Tribulation, those *believers* who manage to survive the Tribulation will be miraculously transported to Jerusalem from all parts of the world by thousands of God's angels.[16] There Christ will apportion out His kingdom blessings to both resurrected saints from heaven and nonresurrected Tribulation survivors.[17] The various localities and responsibilities will be assigned primarily on the basis of Christian faithfulness and perhaps secondarily on the basis of personal choice of geographical regions.[18] Those are the days when "many who are first shall be last, and the last first."[19] For a thousand years Christ and His many human subordinates will rule the world in peace and justice.[20] The headquarters of government will be in Jerusalem,[21] and Palestine with its enlarged borders will be the most prominent nation in the world[22] (though not necessarily the largest in population).

The Millennium

The nonresurrected Tribulation survivors will marry and bear children, leading lives that are somewhat similar to our own today, except idealized in every respect.[23] As the centuries of the Millennium roll on, a minority of children born into this idyllic world will foolishly reject Christ as their Savior, and these rebels will in turn marry, bear children, and establish Christ-rejecting families of their own. This rebellious minority will continue to grow until its numbers are "as the sand of the sea."[24]

At the end of the Millennium, Satan will be temporarily released from the abyss in which he will have been confined for the duration of the Millennium, and he will lead a vast horde of rebels in a mass revolution against the seat of government in Jerusalem.[25] The unarmed believers in Jerusalem will be defended by God Himself as He sends fire from heaven to destroy all the rebels on the spot.[26] Satan will be thrown permanently into the lake of fire, and no created being will ever again rise up to challenge his Creator.[27]

The New World

After this will be the resurrection of the lost of all ages, followed by God's Great White Throne judgment.[28] Here every lost person will receive his equitable sentence in hell forever.[29] Then God will destroy our earth and solar system (and perhaps the entire universe as well) with a tremendous holocaust of fire, and a perfect new earth and sky will take their place.[30] The heavenly city will become even more beautiful than it was before as it descends from God's heaven to the new earth[31] and rests on twelve overlaying foundations made of exceptionally precious minerals.[32]

The technical kingship of the new world will pass from Christ to God the Father,[33] though Christ and His millennial officers will continue to reign forever in a subordinate sense.[34] The eternal new world will have no physical sun or tangible temple, since God Himself will be the Source of all light and the Center of all worship.[35] All tears will be gone forever, since there will be nothing to cry about in God's perfect new universe.[36]

River of Life

From God's throne in the New Jerusalem will flow "a river of the water of life, clear as crystal."[37] Adjacent to the river will be "the tree of life, bearing twelve kinds of fruit."[38] This setting is similar to the millennial river-and-tree scene described in Ezekiel 47:1-12, since God's eternal *new* world is really a continuation and upgrading of the thousand-year *millennial* world.

A careful study of the eternal *new* world as described in Revelation 21 and 22 shows a number of features which are somewhat similar to the *millennial* world as described in the Old Testament. One of these interesting similarities is the tree of life, with its twelve kinds of fruit and its healing leaves (compare Ezekiel 47:12). In Ezekiel 47:12 the leaves are "for healing" (that is, for the healing of the battered survivors of the Tribulation), while in Revelation 22:2 "the leaves of the tree were for the healing of the nations," (that is, for the healing of the nations disrupted at the end of the Millennium by the Satan-led rebellion). In other words, early in the history of the new world God will heal all the scars left behind by the rebels of the Millennium.

Cure for the Curse

Even though Christ's millennial kingdom on earth will have been idyllic in most ways, the age-old curse initiated by Adam's sin will apparently have been lifted only partially, since the nonresurrected people of the Millennium will not yet be absolutely immortal, and since the world itself will need to be renovated by fire. But in God's eternal new world the curse of Adam's sin will be *completely* lifted: "There shall no longer be any curse."[39] No physical decay or death of any kind will pollute God's perfect new world. All living things will stay young and healthy forever, and the infamous "second law of thermodynamics" will plague us no more.

It is the curse of this second law of thermodynamics that causes all systems in our present universe to become less orderly as time goes on, unless something or someone works hard at maintaining order. This is why the engine in your new car will eventually need repairs, and why the lawn in front of your house will need periodic weeding, watering, and feeding in order to keep both you and your neighbors happy with its appearance!

But in God's new world there will be no second law of thermodynamics. All processes of every kind will continue to operate in perfect order at all times. All electrical, chemical, and mechanical processes will be free of wasted energy given off in unrecoverable heat, light, sound, or any other form of energy. The eternal new world will truly be the engineers' and scientists' delight!

The Laws of Life

But even though the law of deterioration will be abolished forever, we do not believe that *every* law of physics will be repealed. Remember that God established most of His laws of physics and nature long before Adam and Eve sinned, and that almost all of God's laws of nature are a blessing to us rather than a curse.

The law of gravity, for example, is a tremendous boon to mankind. Without this law we wouldn't be able to drive a car, walk down the street, or even lie down to sleep! Without this law even eating would be a hard job, as all the astronauts have learned. We believe that the settlement of the New Jerusalem onto its twelve layered foundations[40] suggests strongly that this useful law of gravity will remain in effect even in God's eternal new world. The flowing river described in Revelation 22:1,2 provides further evidence that gravity will be at work in the new world, for without the pull of gravity, water would disperse randomly rather than flow in a river channel.

Even time itself will not be completely eliminated in eternity, for the tree of life will bear twelve kinds of fruit, one for every *month* of the year.[41] Even in eternity there will be regularly recurring events! Our eternal life will not consist of an ethereal, timeless dream, but it will contain a great variety of both scheduled and spontaneous events. We will always be looking forward to new vistas of education, worship, and service.

Drink and Live

The beauty of the new world will certainly eclipse our most spectacular scenic wonders today, and some of our time will be spent exploring the scenic beauties of this newly created earth and sky.

Yet the physical handiwork of God will not be our greatest source of enjoyment in eternity. What we will enjoy most will be our unbroken fellowship with the millions or billions of believers and angels in heaven, and especially our fellowship with the triune God Himself.[42] For every true believer this will be the ultimate joy of time or eternity, while for every unbeliever this lost fellowship will be the greatest catastrophe of the universe. Christ's offer of eternal life is waiting for you right now: "Whosoever will, let him take the water of life freely."[43] Take this offer of life now, while you still have the opportunity!

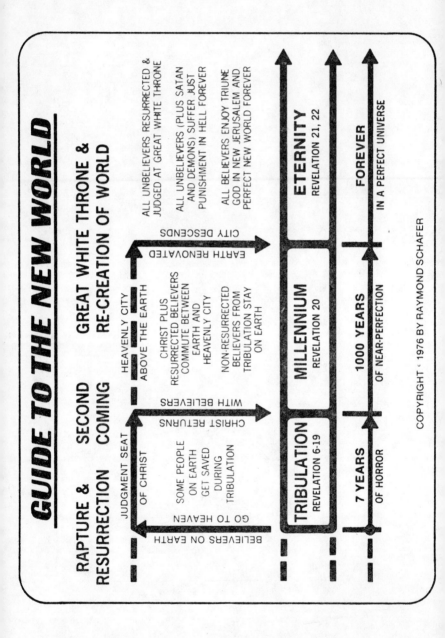

GUIDE TO THE NEW WORLD

RAPTURE & RESURRECTION

SECOND COMING

GREAT WHITE THRONE & RE-CREATION OF WORLD

JUDGMENT SEAT OF CHRIST

SOME PEOPLE ON EARTH GET SAVED DURING TRIBULATION

CHRIST RETURNS — WITH BELIEVERS

BELIEVERS ON EARTH — GO TO HEAVEN

HEAVENLY CITY ABOVE THE EARTH

CHRIST PLUS RESURRECTED BELIEVERS COMMUTE BETWEEN EARTH AND HEAVENLY CITY

NON-RESURRECTED BELIEVERS FROM TRIBULATION STAY ON EARTH

CITY DESCENDS

EARTH RENOVATED

ALL UNBELIEVERS RESURRECTED & JUDGED AT GREAT WHITE THRONE

ALL UNBELIEVERS (PLUS SATAN AND DEMONS) SUFFER JUST PUNISHMENT IN HELL FOREVER

ALL BELIEVERS ENJOY TRIUNE GOD IN NEW JERUSALEM AND PERFECT NEW WORLD FOREVER

TRIBULATION Revelation 6-19	MILLENNIUM Revelation 20	ETERNITY Revelation 21, 22
7 YEARS OF HORROR	1000 YEARS OF NEAR-PERFECTION	FOREVER IN A PERFECT UNIVERSE

COPYRIGHT © 1976 BY RAYMOND SCHAFER

RECOMMENDED READING

Major Bible Passages (listed in order of recommended reading)

- Books of 1 and 2 Thessalonians
- Matthew chapters 24 and 25
- 1 Corinthians chapter 15
- Psalm 72
- Isaiah chapters 11, 12, 35
- Book of Revelation

Other Books (listed alphabetically by author's last name)

Graham, Billy, *Angels: God's Secret Agents* (Doubleday, 1975).

Lindsey, Hal, *The Late Great Planet Earth* (Zondervan, 1973).

Lindsey, Hal, *There's a New World Coming* (Vision, 1973).

Pentecost, J. Dwight, *Things to Come* (Dunham-Zondervan, 1958).

Ryrie, Charles C., *The Basis of the Premillennial Faith* (Loizeaux, 1953).

Ryrie, Charles C., *Revelation* (Moody, 1968).

Unger, Merrill F., *Biblical Demonology* (Victor Books, 1952).

Walvoord, John F., *The Millennial Kingdom* (Dunham-Zondervan, 1969).

Walvoord, John F., *The Nations in Prophecy* (Zondervan, 1967).

Walvoord, John F., *The Rapture Question* (Dunham-Zondervan, 1957).

Walvoord, John F., *The Revelation of Jesus Christ* (Moody, 1966).

Weldon, John, and Levitt, Zola, *UFO's: What on Earth Is Happening?* (Harvest, 1975).

FOOTNOTES

Chapter 1
THE SHOUT!

1. 1 Thessalonians 1:9, 10.
2. Philippians 3:20.
3. John 14:2, 3.
4. John 21:22.
5. Romans 13:11, 12.
6. Luke 19:12, 13 KJV.
7. Revelation 22:20 KJV; cp. 22:7, 12; 3:11.
8. Revelation 22:20 KJV.
9. 1 Thessalonians 4:13-18.
10. See Matthew 27:50-53 for an additional hint of this reunion.
11. John 20:28.
12. Samuel Stennett.
13. Matthew 24:19; Mark 13:17; Luke 21:23.
14. 2 Thessalonians 2:11, 12.
15. Hebrews 3:7, 8, 15; 4:7 RKJV.

Chapter 2
FOREVER YOUNG

1. Job 19:25-27 RKJV.
2. John 11:24.
3. Psalm 16:10 NASB margin.
4. Daniel 12:2.
5. Lazarus: John 11:38-45. Widow's son: Luke 7:11-16. Shunammite woman's son: 2 Kings 4:18-37. Corpse on Elijah: 2 Kings 13:20, 21. Ruler's daughter: Matthew 9:18-26; Mark 5:21-42; Luke 8:41-56. Plus numerous other raisings—see Hebrews 11:35.
6. 1 Corinthians 15:23.

7. 1 Corinthians 15:37, 38, 42-44.

8. 1 Corinthians 15:47-49.

9. 1 Corinthians 15:41, 42.

10. Daniel 12:3.

11. Hebrews 11:35.

12. Matthew 5:8, 10, 12.

13. 1 John 2:28; 1 Corinthians 3:15; 9:27; Romans 14:12; 2 Corinthians 5:10.

14. 2 Timothy 2:12; Revelation 5:9, 10; 20:4, 6; Luke 19:11-27.

15. Daniel 12:3.

16. John 20:14-16.

17. Luke 24:18 KJV.

18. John 21:1-7.

19. John 20:26; Luke 24:30, 31, 36, 50, 51; Acts 1:9.

20. Luke 24:15-50; John 20:15 – 21:22; 1 Corinthians 15:3-8.

21. Luke 22:29, 30; Matthew 26:29; Revelation 19:7-9.

22. Luke 24:36-53; John 21:1-22.

23. Luke 16:9.

24. John 15:12, 17; 17:21, 23, 24; 1 John 3:11, 23; 4:11, 12, 16-21.

25. Galatians 3:28; 1 Corinthians 1:10-13; Romans 15:5, 6.

26. Genesis 2:18-24.

27. Genesis 1:27, 28; 9:1.

28. Ephesians 5:22-33; 2 Corinthians 11:2.

29. Matthew 22:30.

30. John 20:15, 26-28; Luke 24:18.

31. Genesis 2:21-23; ep. 3:1-6.

32. 1 Timothy 2:8-14; 1 Corinthians 14:34-37.

33. Galatians 3:28.

34. John 20:15, 26, 27; Revelation 1:12-16.

35. Genesis 2:25.

36. 2 Corinthians 3:18; 4:6; Hebrews 2:9; Psalm 45:1, 2.

37. Anne Ross Cousin.

38. 1 John 4:7.

39. Revelation 21:4; 22:3-5.

Chapter 3
LIFE IN THE SKY

1. Genesis 12:1, 2.
2. Hebrews 11:8.
3. Wealth: Genesis 13:2,6; 24:1. Fellowship and fatherhood: Genesis 18:17-33; 12:2, 3, 7; 13:14-18; 14:18-20; 15:1-21; 17:1-11; 21:1-7; 22:16-18.
4. Hebrews 11:9, 10.
5. Hebrews 11:16.
6. 2 Peter 3:10-13; Revelation 21:1.
7. Revelation 21:2, 10-27; 22:1-5.
8. Hebrews 11:10; cp. 11:16; 12:22, 27, 28.
9. Hebrews 12:22-24.
10. Anne Ross Cousin.
11. Psalm 45:8; Revelation 21:21.
12. Hebrews 11:14-16.
13. Revelation 21:16.
14. Romans 8:18-21; Isaiah 35:1-10.
15. Revelation 22:2.
16. Revelation 21:18-21.
17. Genesis 1:28.
18. Revelation 5:11-14; Hebrews 12:22; 1:6; Job 38:4-7.
19. Ephesians 6:11, 12; Mark 5:1-13, esp. vv. 9, 13.
20. Jude 6, 7.
21. Revelation 21:17; Genesis 32:24-29; 18:1-22; Hebrews 13:2.
22. Idol statues: 1 Corinthians 10:20. People: Matthew 12:43-45. Animals: Matthew 8:30-32.
23. Spirit (capacity to worship God): Revelation 5:11-14; Hebrews 1:6. Soul (rational personality): Revelation 10:9-11; 17:1-3; 18:1-3, 21; 20:1-3; 22:8, 9. Body: Revelation 21:17; Genesis 32:24-29; 18:1-22. Immortality: Luke 20:35, 36.
24. Matthew 22:30; Mark 12:25.
25. Genesis 3:24; Exodus 25:17-22; Ezekiel 10:1-19; 11:22, 23.

26. Isaiah 6:1-7.

27. Matthew 18:10; Hebrews 1:14; Psalm 91:9-12.

28. Job 1:6; Matthew 18:10.

29. Abraham: Genesis 18:1-5. Isaiah: Isaiah 6:5-7. John: Revelation 10:9; 19:10; 22:8-10.

30. Revelation 19:9, 10; 22:8, 9.

31. Jude 6.

32. Psalm 91:11.

33. Hebrews 1:14.

34. Philippians 1:23 KJV.

35. 1 Thessalonians 4:16, 17; 1 Corinthians 15:3-58, esp. vv. 17-20, 23, 52.

36. 1 Samuel 28:7-14.

37. Matthew 17:1-4; Mark 9:2-5; Luke 9:28-33.

38. Luke 16:19-31, esp. vv. 22-24.

39. 1 John 3:2; 1 Corinthians 15:41-43; Daniel 12:3.

40. Luke 24:13-29.

41. 2 Timothy 2:11, 12; Luke 19:12-19; Revelation 5:9, 10; 20:6.

42. Genesis 1:26, 27; 9:6.

43. 2 Corinthians 5:1-4.

44. 1 Corinthians 15:35-57; Revelation 20:6.

45. Romans 12:1, 2; 6:11-19; Galatians 5:16-25.

46. John 10:27-30; Book of 1 John.

47. 1 John 1:9.

48. Hebrews 12:1-13.

49. Hebrews 12:7.

50. Romans 14:10; 1 Corinthians 3:11-15; 2 Corinthians 5:10.

51. 1 Corinthians 3:15.

52. Philippians 3:14.

53. Crowns: 1 Corinthians 9:25; 2 Timothy 4:8; James 1:12; 1 Peter 5:4; Revelation 2:10. Cities: Luke 19:11-19.

54. Revelation 19:7, 9.

55. Luke 24:30, 41-43; John 21:9-13.

56. Proverbs 15:13, 15; 17:22; Luke 15:22-24, 32.

57. Revelation 13:15-17.
58. Revelation 15:2; 20:4.
59. Revelation 14:9-11.

Chapter 4
I SEE, I SEE

1. Genesis 3:1-6.
2. Genesis 3:7-10.
3. Implied by Genesis 3:17-19.
4. Genesis 3:8, 9, 14, 15, 21.
5. Oral form: to Adam, Cain, Enoch, Noah, Job, Abraham, Isaac, Jacob, Moses, Joshua, and many prophets (and perhaps many other patriarchs). Written form: in the Holy Scriptures from Genesis to Revelation. (The Book of Job, written before the time of Abraham, was probably the first written Scripture.) Personal form: birth, life, death, resurrection, and return of Christ.
6. Colossians 1:15; John 1:1-5, 14-18; Hebrews 1:1-6.
7. John 16:13-15; 1 Corinthians 2:6-16.
8. 1 Corinthians 13:12.
9. 1 Peter 1:12.
10. Matthew 24:36; Mark 13:32.
11. Romans 11:33-36.
12. 1 Corinthians 13:12.
13. Revelation 6:9-11.
14. Matthew 21:42-44; Mark 11:17; Luke 4:16-21; John 10:31-38; and numerous other Scriptures.
15. Luke 16:25-31.
16. 1 Samuel 28:15-20.
17. Revelation 6:1, 3, 5, 7; 10:9, 11; 11:1-10; 14:6-12, 15-18; 17:1, 2, 7-18; 18:1-3; 21:9; 22:6-10.
18. J. Kent.
19. Ancient crusaders' hymn adapted for post-Reformation believers.
20. Revelation 5:13.

21. Revelation 6:9-11; 15:1-4.
22. 1 Samuel 28:16-19; Luke 16:25-31; 9:28-31.
23. John 15:15.
24. Luke 16:25
25. Luke 16:26.
26. Revelation 6:9-11; 15:1-4.

Chapter 5
WARRIOR FROM HEAVEN

1. Matthew 21:40, 41; Mark 12:9; Luke 20:15, 16; John 3:36; 2 Thessalonians 1:7-10.
2. Isaiah 53:3-7; Matthew 26:47-54, 59-68; 27:11-14, 27-31, 34, 39-44; Luke 23:33, 34.
3. 2 Thessalonians 1:7-10; Revelation 19:11-15.
4. John 1:10, 11; Isaiah 53:3; Matthew 7:13, 14.
5. 2 Thessalonians 1:8 RKJV.
6. Isaiah 61:2; cp. 34:8; Luke 21:20-22.
7. Jeremiah 30:7 KJV; cp. vv. 5, 6.
8. Matthew 24:21.
9. Revelation 6:15-17.
10. Revelation 16:18-20; 6:14.
11. Revelation 6:5-8; Matthew 24:7, 8; Luke 21:10, 11.
12. Seventy-five percent survivors in Revelation 6:8 times 67% survivors in Revelation 9:18 equals 50 percent survivors overall, or an overall death statistic of 50 percent. In addition, many people will die because of the bitter waters mentioned in Revelation 8:11.
13. 2 Thessalonians 1:7-9; Matthew 13:40-42; 25:31-46.
14. John Weldon and Zola Levitt, *UFO's: What on Earth Is Happening?* (Irvine, CA: Harvest House, 1975).
15. Revelation 7:4-10.
16. Matthew 24:9, 10, 15-21; Revelation 6:9, 10; 7:13-17.
17. 1 Thessalonians 2:6, 7.
18. 2 Thessalonians 2:3, 4; Matthew 24:15; Daniel 11:31.
19. Revelation 13:16-18.
20. Revelation 13:17.

21. Revelation 14:13; 15:2-4; Matthew 24:9.
22. Revelation 6:13; 8:8-11; Luke 21:25. (*Astēr*, the Greek word for "star," can refer to any heavenly body except the sun or moon. Right now there are over 50,000 large and small asteroids in orbit around our sun, plus many thousands of meteorites.)
23. Revelation 8:7; 6:14; 16:20.
24. Revelation 6:12, 15-17; 8:12.
25. Revelation 9:20, 21; 16:9-11.
26. Revelation 16:12, 14, 16; Daniel 11:40-45.
27. Daniel 11:40-45.
28. Matthew 24:27; Luke 17:24; 2 Thessalonians 1:7-10; Revelation 19:11-15.
29. Revelation 1:7; Matthew 24:30.
30. Revelation 14:17-20; cp. 19:15.
31. Revelation 19:20, 21; Matthew 7:21-23.
32. Matthew 7:22 RKJV.
33. Matthew 7:23 RKJV.
34. Matthew 25:31-46.
35. Jude 14, 15 RKJV.
36. Revelation 19:15.
37. Matthew 8:38.

Chapter 6
KING OF THE WORLD

1. Copyright © 1953 by S. K. Hine. Assigned to Manna Music, Inc. Copyright © 1955 by Manna Music, Inc. International copyright secured. Printed in U.S.A. All rights reserved.
2. Genesis 1:28.
3. Genesis 3:1-19; Romans 5:12-19.
4. See also 1 Corinthians 15:20-22, 45-49; Hebrews 2:5-15.
5. Psalm 72:1-11.
6. Revelation 20:6; see also vv. 2, 3, 4, 5, 7.
7. Compare Genesis 8:18-21 with Zechariah 14:9; Isaiah 2:2, 3; Psalm 72:1-17.

8. Psalm 29:2 RKJV.
9. Matthew 6:10 RKJV.
10. Psalm 24:9, 10 RKJV.
11. Psalm 29:1, 2 RKJV.
12. Psalm 45:2, 6, 17 RKJV.
13. Psalm 48:1, 2 KJV.
14. Psalm 65:1 KJV.
15. Psalm 115:1 RKJV.
16. Isaac Watts (taken from Psalm 72).
17. Psalm 145:1-5, 10-13 RKJV.
18. Ezekiel 40:2—43:17; cp. 45:1-8.
19. Zechariah 14:16-19; Isaiah 66:18-23.
20. Psalm 22:27, 28; 72:1-11, 17-19; Isaiah 2:1-4.
21. Genesis 3:21.
22. Genesis 4:3-5; 8:20, 21; 12:8; Exodus 12:1-14; 1 Peter 1:18-20; Hebrews 10:1-4.
23. Hebrews 10:1-10.
24. Luke 22:7-20; Mark 14:12-25; 1 Corinthians 11:23-26.
25. Isaiah 11:9.

Chapter 7
MY TEN CITIES

1. 1 Corinthians 9:25, 24.
2. Hebrews 12:1 KJV.
3. Hebrews 12:2-4.
4. 2 Timothy 2:12 RKJV.
5. Revelation 5:10 RKJV.
6. Mark 10:31 RKJV; cp. Matthew 19:30; 20:16; Luke 13:30.
7. Matthew 6:1 RKJV; cp. vv. 2-4.
8. 1 Corinthians 4:5; Romans 14:7-13.
9. Romans 12:1, 2.
10. Ephesians 2:4, 5, 7-9.
11. Luke 17:10.
12. 2 Thessalonians 1:7-10; Jude 14, 15; Revelation 19:11-14.

13. Revelation 5:9, 10; 20:6.
14. Luke 19:11-19; 22:28-30; Matthew 19:27-29.
15. Luke 19:16, 17 RKJV.
16. Isaiah 2:2, 3; 66:18-23; Psalm 48:1-14; 87:1-7.
17. Psalm 22:27, 28; 72:7-11, 17; 86:9, 10; Isaiah 66:10-23.
18. Psalm 72:8-11; Isaiah 66:19, 20; Zechariah 14:16-19.
19. Psalm 22:27, 28; 72:5, 9-11, 15, 17, 19; 86:9; Isaiah 2:2, 3.
20. 1 Peter 1:3, 4.
21. 1 Corinthians 15:41-44; Hebrews 11:35.
22. John 20:14, 15; 21:4; Luke 24:15, 16, 18.
23. Isaiah 65:17-23; 11:6, 8.
24. Numbers 32:1-33; cp. Joshua 13:1—22:9.
25. Psalm 72:1-7, 12-14, 17; 145:13-20; Isaiah 40:9-11.
26. Psalm 72:1-8, 12-14, 17 (NASB marginal wordings in vv. 2, 3, 4, 5, 6, 7; alt. in v. 8).

Chapter 8
NO MORE MEDICARE

1. Isaiah 11:6-9 TLB.
2. Genesis 3:17, 18; Romans 8:20-22.
3. Romans 8:19-21.
4. Romans 8:21; Isaiah 65:17-25.
5. Genesis 3:19; 5:5, 8, 11, 14, 17, 20, 27, 31; Romans 5:12-21; 8:18-23; 1 Thessalonians 4:13-18; 1 Corinthians 15:3-58, esp. vv. 20-23, 45-57.
6. Genesis 3:21.
7. Genesis 5:3-5.
8. Methuselah, 969 years: Genesis 5:27. Jared, 962 years: Genesis 5:20. Noah, 950 years: Genesis 9:29.
9. Note the decreasing lifespans (with only temporary exceptions) in Genesis 5:5, 8, 11, 14, 17, 20, 27, 31.
10. Genesis 11:10-25.
11. For example, Terah, the father of Abraham, died at 205 years (Genesis 11:32; cp. vv. 24-27).

12. Genesis 11:24. Note the other low ages of parenthood in Genesis 11:12-22.

13. Isaiah 65:20-22.

14. 1 Corinthians 15:51-54; Luke 20:34-38; 1 Thessalonians 4:13-18; Revelation 22:3-5.

15. Isaiah 65:22 TLB.

16. Isaiah 65:20 TLB.

17. Romans 8:19-23; Isaiah 35:1-10; cp. 11:1-9; 65:17-25.

18. Matthew 22:30; Mark 12:25; Luke 20:35.

19. Genesis 1:28; cp. 9:7.

20. Isaiah 65:20 NASB.

21. Isaiah 35:1-7; cp. 41:18, 19; 51:3.

22. Isaiah 65:21-23; Micah 4:1-4.

23. Jeremiah 31:6-9; Isaiah 35:5, 6.

24. Genesis 9:2.

25. Isaiah 11:6, 8, 9.

26. Isaiah 11:7; 65:25.

27. Genesis 1:30.

28. Luke 24:30, 42, 43; John 21:9-13.

29. Matthew 22:30; Mark 12:25; Luke 20:35.

30. Isaiah 35:1, 2 TLB.

31. Ezekiel 47:1, 2, 7, 8, 12.

32. Ezekiel 47:8.

33. Ezekiel 47:9, 10.

34. Zechariah 3:10 TLB.

35. Isaiah 35:5, 6.

36. Matthew 11:5; 12:15; 14:14.

37. Jeremiah 31:6-9; Isaiah 35:5, 6.

38. Romans 8:20-23.

39. Micah 4:3; cp. Isaiah 2:4; Joel 3:10.

40. Micah 4:3 TLB.

41. Isaiah 2:2, 3; 66:18-23; Psalm 48:1-14; 87:1-7.

42. Zechariah 14:9; Psalm 22:27, 28; 72:1-17; 86:9; Isaiah 2:1-4.

43. Katharine Lee Bates.

44. Revelation 3:10; 1 Thessalonians 1:10; 4:13-18; John 14:1-3.
45. 2 Thessalonians 1:7-10; Jude 14, 15; Revelation 5:8-10; 21:6.
46. Martyrs: Matthew 24:9; Revelation 6:9; 14:13. Survivors: Matthew 24:13, 16-21, 31, 36-41; Revelation 12:6, 13, 14-17.
47. Revelation 6:9-11; 7:9-17; 14:1-5, 12, 13; 15:1-3.
48. Revelation 20:4.
49. Matthew 24:31; 25:31-40; Isaiah 35:3-10; 65:17-25.
50. 2 Thessalonians 2:7-12.

Chapter 9
SUPER-RIOT

1. Ezekiel 28:12-15; Isaiah 14:12-14; Job 38:6, 7.
2. Isaiah 14:13, 14.
3. Matthew 25:41; Revelation 12:7-9.
4. Isaiah 14:12.
5. Psalm 103:19-22; 148:5-13; Isaiah 40:12-26; Romans 9:20, 21; 1 Timothy 1:17; 6:14-16.
6. Revelation 20:10.
7. 1 Corinthians 10:19, 20.
8. Matthew 4:23, 24; 16:28; 17:14-18; Mark 1:32-34; 5:1-9; Luke 8:26-30.
9. Matthew 8:31, 32; Mark 5:11-13; Luke 8:32, 33.
10. Revelation 7:9-12; 19:16-21; 20:10-15.
11. Ephesians 6:12.
12. Direct assault: 1 Peter 5:8, 9; Ephesians 6:16; 1 Thessalonians 2:18. Deception: Ephesians 6:11; John 8:44; Genesis 3:1-5. Religious imitation: 2 Corinthians 11:13-15; 1 Timothy 4:1-3.
13. 1 Timothy 4:1.
14. John 3:36; 8:24, 25; 2 Thessalonians 2:8-12; Revelation 21:8.
15. Ephesians 6:10-18; 1 John 4:1-4.
16. Revelation 13:15-17.

17. Revelation 14:12, 13; 15:2; cp. Matthew 24:9.
18. Matthew 24:21, 22.
19. Revelation 19:11-21, esp. vv. 20, 21; 2 Thessalonians 1:7-10; Jude 14, 15; Psalm 96:12, 13.
20. Revelation 20:1-3.
21. The world: 1 John 2:15-17; 5:4, 5; James 1:27; 4:4. The flesh: Galatians 5:16-24; Romans 6:11-18. The devil: Ephesians 4:27; 6:11-16; James 4:7.
22. Job 1:6-12; 1 Thessalonians 2:18; Luke 22:3; John 13:26, 27; see also Matthew 4:1-11; Luke 4:1-13.
23. Ephesians 6:12.
24. Revelation 20:1-3.
25. Psalm 72; Isaiah chapters 11, 35, 65:17-25.
26. 1 John 1:8, 10; Galatians 5:17-21; Romans 6:12—7:25.
27. 1 John 1:8, 10 RKJV.
28. Romans 3:10-23.
29. 1 John 3:2 KJV.
30. Isaiah 2:4; Zechariah 14:16-19; Psalm 72:12-14.
31. Psalm 2, esp. v. 12.
32. Psalm 2.
33. Revelation 20:11-15.
34. Revelation 20:8.
35. Psalm 2:3.
36. Psalm 2:10-12; 72:9, 15; Revelation 19:10.
37. Psalm 72:1-4, 12-14.
38. Psalm 2:1-3.
39. Psalm 2:4-12.
40. Psalms 72, 87; Isaiah 2:2-4; 11:4, 5.
41. Psalm 72:4, 9, 11; Isaiah 11:4; Revelation 19:15.
42. Isaiah 11:4; 65:20 NASB, TLB; Psalm 2:12.
43. Isaiah 35:8-10; 65:18, 19; Revelation 15:3, 4; 19:1-3.
44. Psalm 2:1-3; Revelation 20:8, 9; cp. Luke 4:28, 29; John 7:1, 25, 30, 44; 11:53; 19:6, 7.
45. Revelation 20:7-9.
46. Revelation 20:9.
47. Revelation 20:10.

Chapter 10
GUILTY!

1. Hebrews 9:27 KJV.
2. 1 John 4:16; cp. vv. 7-19; John 3:16, 17.
3. 1 John 1:5 KJV; cp. Isaiah 6:1-7; Psalm 29:2; 30:4; 47:8; 48:1; 60:6; 89:35; 93:5; Exodus 19:10-25; 20:1-19.
4. Revelation 4:8; cp. Isaiah 6:1-4.
5. 1 Peter 1:18, 19; 2:21-25; 3:18; Ephesians 1:7; 2:4-9.
6. John 3:36; cp. 3:14-18.
7. Revelation 20:11-15; 21:8.
8. Revelation 16:5-7; cp. 14:7, 9, 10; 15:1-4; 19:1-6.
9. 2 Peter 3:9; Revelation 22:17; 2 Corinthians 5:20, 21; John 3:14-17.
10. Daniel 12:2 RKJV.
11. Revelation 20:12, 13.
12. Daniel 12:3.
13. Psalm 139:13-16.
14. Revelation 20:12,13.
15. Revelation 21:8; 22:15; Galatians 5:19-21.
16. Revelation 20:13; 2 Peter 2:1-3; Jude 4-15.
17. John 3:16-18, 35, 36.
18. Romans 3:23 KJV.
19. Titus 3:5, 6 RKJV; cp. Ephesians 1:7; 2:8, 9.
20. Romans 3:10-23.
21. Romans 5:12.
22. Galatians 5:19-21; Romans 6:16-21.
23. Galatians 5:19-21.
24. Psalm 139:1-4.
25. God: Romans 3:10-23. The natives: Romans 2:12-15.
26. Romans 1:18-23.
27. Romans 1:19, 20.
28. Romans 2:14, 15.
29. 1 Timothy 4:1, 2.

30. Retarding of worldwide sin: 2 Thessalonians 2:6, 7. Influencing to repent: Acts 17:30; 2 Peter 3:9.

31. Abraham: Genesis 15:1-6. Naaman: 2 Kings 5:1-15, esp. v. 15. Nebuchadnezzar: Daniel 4:1-37, esp. vv. 2, 3, 34-37. Doctrinal summary: Romans 4:1-10; Acts 10:34, 35.

32. Romans 1:18-23.

33. Matthew 7:13, 14; Romans 1:18-32.

34. Romans 10:14, 15; Acts 1:8; Matthew 28:19, 20.

35. Acts 2:1-41, esp. v. 41; Acts 4:1-4; 5:15; 14:1; 16:5; 17:1-4, 10-12.

36. 2 Timothy 2:24-26.

37. 1 Corinthians 15:3, 4; 1 Peter 1:18-21; 3:18; Romans 4:24, 25.

38. John 3:16-18, 35, 36.

39. John 3:16-18, 35, 36.

40. James 2:19 KJV.

41. Revelation 20:12.

42. Revelation 20:12.

43. Revelation 20:13; 21:8; 1 Corinthians 6:9, 10; Galatians 5:19-21.

44. Revelation 20:13; Romans 2:1-16; Deuteronomy 24:16.

45. John 3:16-18, 35, 36.

46. Revelation 20:12.

47. Philippians 4:3; Revelation 3:5; 21:27.

48. Revelation 13:7, 8; 20:15.

49. Revelation 20:15.

50. 2 Thessalonians 1:7-9; Jude 12, 13; Matthew 25:41; John 3:16-18, 35, 36.

51. Revelation 20:12.

52. Luke 12:47, 48 RKJV.

53. Matthew 10:15; 11:23, 24; Mark 6:11; Luke 10:12.

54. Matthew 11:21, 22; Luke 10:13, 14.

55. Romans 2:1-29, esp. vv. 12, 14-16, 26, 27.

56. Luke 16:23-25.

57. Matthew 8:12; 13:40-42; 22:13; 24:51; 25:30; Luke 13:28.

58. Luke 16:24 KJV.
59. Revelation 20:15; 21:8; cp. 19:20; 20:10.
60. 2 Peter 3:9; Revelation 22:17; 2 Corinthians 5:20, 21; John 3:14-17.

Chapter 11
HAPPY NEW WORLD

1. This judgmental cataclysm is hinted at in Ezekiel 28:11-19 and Isaiah 14:12-15.
2. 2 Peter 3:7, 10-14.
3. 2 Peter 3:13 RKJV; cp. Revelation 20:11—21:5.
4. Revelation 21:3, 4.
5. Revelation 21:3, 22, 23; 22:3, 4.
6. 1 Corinthians 15:23-28; Hebrews 1:8; Revelation 11:5; 22:3-5.
7. Philippians 2:5-11; Revelation 20:6; Psalms 1 and 72.
8. Revelation 22:3, 4.
9. Revelation 21:2.
10. Revelation 21:2.
11. Revelation 21:16.
12. Revelation 21:14, 19, 20.
13. Revelation 21:17, 18.
14. Revelation 21:22, 23.
15. Hebrews 11:10, 16; 12:22, 27, 28.
16. Revelation 21:24-26.
17. Revelation 21:12.
18. Revelation 21:14.
19. Revelation 21:24-26.
20. Psalm 19:1 KJV.
21. Revelation 4:11.
22. Luke 16:23; cp. vv. 24-31.
23. Revelation 22:14, 15; cp. Matthew 8:10-12; Jude 12, 13; 2 Peter 2:12-17.

Chapter 12
FOREVER ALIVE

1. Luke 16:22, 9.
2. 2 Corinthians 5:1-4; cp. Luke 16:23; Matthew 17:1-4.
3. Philippians 1:21-23; Matthew 6:19-21.
4. 1 Thessalonians 4:13-18.
5. 1 Thessalonians 4:16, 17; 1:9, 10; John 14:1-3; Philippians 3:20, 21; 1 Corinthians 15:51-57.
6. 1 Thessalonians 4:14-16; 1 Corinthians 15:51-54.
7. 1 Thessalonians 4:17.
8. John 14:1-3; Hebrews 11:10, 16; 12:22, 23.
9. See Chapter 7 under "Highways to Heaven" heading.
10. Revelation 21:1, 2, 10.
11. Jews and church in city: Revelation 21:12, 14. Nations outside city proper, in new earth: Revelation 21:24, 26.
12. Revelation 6:1—20:3; Matthew 24:3—25:46; Isaiah 24:1-23.
13. Revelation 6:8 and 9:18 show an aggregate death statistic of 50 percent (see Chapter 5, note 12).
14. 2 Thessalonians 1:7-10; Jude 14, 15; Revelation 19:11-15, 19-21.
15. Revelation 6:9-11; 15:2-4.
16. Matthew 24:30, 31; Mark 13:26, 27; Jeremiah 31:6-9; Isaiah 11:10-12.
17. Resurrected saints: Matthew 19:28, 29; Revelation 20:4-6. Nonresurrected survivors: Luke 19:11-19; Matthew 25:31-36.
18. Faithfulness: Luke 19:11-19; Matthew 19:28, 29. Choice: Numbers 32:1-33.
19. Mark 10:31 RKJV; cp. Matthew 19:30; Luke 13:29, 30.
20. Revelation 20:4-6; Psalm 72:1-20; Isaiah 11:1-16; 35:1-10; 40:1-31; 60:1—61:11.
21. Isaiah 2:1-3; 24:23; Psalm 48:1-14; 87:1-7.
22. Genesis 15:18-21; Ezekiel 47:13—48:35.
23. Isaiah 65:18-23; 11:6, 8.
24. Revelation 20:8 KJV; cp. Psalm 2:1-6.

25. Revelation 20:7, 8.
26. Revelation 20:9.
27. Revelation 20:10-15; 21:3-8.
28. Revelation 20:11-13; cp. Hebrews 9:27.
29. Revelation 20:14, 15; 21:8; John 3:36; Psalm 9:17.
30. Revelation 21:1; cp. 2 Peter 3:7, 10-13.
31. Revelation 21:2, 10, 11.
32. Revelation 21:14, 19, 20.
33. 1 Corinthians 15:23-28; Revelation 22:3.
34. Revelation 22:3-5; cp. 5:12, 13; 11:15; Hebrews 1:8.
35. Revelation 21:22, 23; 22:5.
36. Revelation 21:4; 22:3.
37. Revelation 22:1.
38. Revelation 22:2.
39. Revelation 22:3.
40. Revelation 21:10, 14, 19, 20.
41. Revelation 22:2
42. Revelation 21:3, 4, 22; 22:3-5; cp. 5:6-14; John 17:24.
43. Revelation 22:17 KJV.

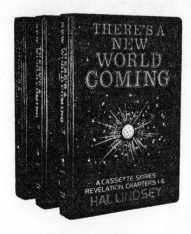